3,000,000 HINDUS

pressed against the crowd-control barriers,
anxious to plunge into the filthy waters of
the Ganges. Today, they believed, the river
would take on magical healing powers. But
the magic would last only a short while.

I had worked as a control guard all
morning long. I had seen many emotions on
the faces of my countrymen—hope,
despair, anxiety. Now I saw something new:
fear. I didn't dare think what might happen
if the crowd panicked.

Then, suddenly, if was happening. The
hordes began to charge like maddened
oxen, oblivious to those who fell
underfoot. . . .

*This book is lovingly dedicated to Mawii
who shares the walk of faith with me
without complaint or flinching.*

THE DIME THAT LASTED FOREVER

. . . .

ROCHUNGA PUDAITE

All Scripture quotations are taken from the King James Version.

Third printing, January 2006

Library of Congress Catalog Card Number 85-50093
ISBN 0-8423-0554-8
© 1985 by Rochunga Pudaite
Printed in the United States of America
Printed by Dickinson Press Inc.

CONTENTS

• • •

FOREWORD

• • •

The tradition of storytelling runs deep among the tribal peoples off northeast India. In the flickering amber light of a fire, villagers gather to tell legends of ancestral heroes and laugh at the folly of mythical simpletons. Tribal and family history has been passed from generation to generation, from grandfather to grandson.

In 1910, the gospel first reached the remote hills of Manipur. My grandfather, Chawnga Pudaite, was one of the first Hmar tribesmen to become a Christian. Soon he became a great preacher, continuing the oral tradition with a new theme, the Good News of Jesus Christ. My father, Rochunga Pudaite, grew up in those hills. As he pursued his education, a task which took him to other parts of India as well as to the British Isles and the United States, he carried with him the storytelling tradition of the Hmar people.

This collection of modern parables has been gathered from the many opportunities my father has had during his ministry to tell people about his experiences—staff meetings of Bibles for the World, family fellowship times, and banquets. He, like my grandfather, has combined his storytelling talents with his passion for the gospel to weave entertaining and spiritually enlightening stories.

It has been my privilege to help him assimilate and edit these parables for the reader, to extend the Hmar oral tradition to another generation and to a new audience.

John Pudaite

GOD'S
HORIZON
• • • • • • • •

Lo, I am with you always,
even unto the end of the world.
Matthew 28:20

My traveling days began when I was a young lad of
ten living in a tribal village in northeastern India. It
was my father who first suggested I leave our village
to travel the ninety-six miles to the Mission School
in Churachandpur, Manipur.

"My son," he told me, "you know we do not have
God's Word in the Hmar language. We have only the
Lushai Bible, and many of our people do not under-
stand it. Someone must translate God's Word into
Hmar and have copies printed so that all of our peo-
ple can read it for themselves."

I understood why my father should feel this way
– he was not only the pastor of our little church in
Phulpui, but he also walked the trails of our district
to bring the gospel to other villages.

"The one who does this work must first become

very educated," he explained. "He will need more knowledge than any Hmar has ever attained. Would you like to be this man?"

I considered this possibility. To become the most educated Hmar there had ever been sounded like a very worthy goal. Just thinking about it made me stand tall and hold my head high. Such a man would receive much respect. Everyone would hold him in high esteem. Certainly he would be the most famous man in all our tribe.

"Father, I think I would like to be an educated man," I solemnly told him.

"We will pray about it."

Later I began thinking about the difficulties involved in obtaining such an education. Only three years of schooling were offered in the small school in our village. To continue learning I would have to walk the ninety-six miles to the mission school. That was farther than I could even imagine. I had been taught that our Mongolian ancestors had traveled from central China across the lower Himalayas and into the foothills of those great mountains. But that was centuries before and very few Hmar in recent memory had ever traveled so far.

I looked down at my legs. They seemed small and frail. The soles of my brown feet were tough from running barefoot all my life, but could they carry me so far? The jungle I would have to cross was a vast, almost impenetrable rainforest covering rugged mountain terrain. Huge, hungry Bengal tigers dwelt in the depths of the forest, as well as bears, python and wild elephants.

The longer I thought about it, the less pleasant the prospect of an education seemed. Even if I managed to survive the six or seven days it would take to walk that far, when I reached my goal I would be separated from all my loved ones. Just thinking about it aroused pangs of loneliness in my chest.

I hurried to our bamboo home to tell my father I had changed my mind. The sight of that secure dwelling reassured my racing heart and I sat down on the front porch next to my father.

"Look, Father," I cried out, "just look how short and puny my legs are. They could never travel all the miles it would take to become educated."

My father contemplated my legs. He turned me all the way around, then ran his fingers up and down my limbs.

"My! What strong muscles you have, my son," he declared. "I had never before noticed how sturdy your legs are." I felt strength coming into my body even as he talked. He smiled at me knowingly and said, "My son, if you were to leave our village to get an education, you would never be alone. The Lord would be with you each step you take away from our home, and each day you are separated from our family."

I was not totally reassured. I wanted someone with me I could see. A few Sundays later my father was preaching, orally translating from the Lushai Bible as he spoke. Part of a verse he used puzzled me, ". . . having loved His own which were in the world, He loved them unto the horizon." (John 13:1) As we walked home after the service, I asked him about it.

"You said God's love is unto the *horizon*. How far is that?"

He replied without much thinking, "I don't know."

I told my father, "If God loves me only as far as I can see, how can I trust Him to be with me in Churachandpur? If you don't know how far the horizon is, I will not go to school!"

Three days later during our meal time, he was quiet, and afterward he sat on our porch gazing into the distance. Finally he asked me to go with him on a hike. We climbed to the top of nearby Sumtuk Mountain.

"Let's climb this tree," he said. From the arms of the spreading branches we could see far across a beautiful valley.

"That is the Cachar Valley," he explained. "It takes many days to journey across such a large valley. Look at that long mountain range beyond the valley. Do you see the tall peak where the sky touches the earth?"

"Yes." I was still puzzled.

"If you were to journey many weeks and come to the top of that mountain and look beyond, you would see another valley, and another mountain range in the distance. If you then journeyed on for many more days and weeks to the second mountain, you would be able to see a third. If you traveled to that you could still see further, for the horizon is never ending, my son. Like the horizon, there is no place in this world where the love of God has not touched or cannot reach.

"When you go to school, whether you are on a mountaintop or in a deep valley, God will still be with you. It is impossible to travel beyond the scope of God's love."

In the branches of that tree, as I stood gazing into the purple haze of that distant mountain, I felt encircled by God's love. I still felt small and insignificant, surely too weak to be the one to take on such a task as translating God's Word. But I now had the assurance that wherever I might go, God would be with me.

As best as I can tabulate it, before completing my university degree I walked more than fifteen thousand miles in and out of our village. Since that time I have traveled around the world many times. I have been privileged to see much of our beautiful planet earth. But I have never traveled alone. God has been with me.

MY BIG GOD

● ● ● ● ● ● ●

My God shall supply all your
need according to His riches in
glory by Christ Jesus.
Philippians 4:19

I continued my studies at Jorhat Christian High School in 1946. Jorhat is in the valley of the neighboring state of Assam, four hundred miles away from my home in Pulpui, Manipur. It was a long journey by foot, boat, bus, train and rickshaw from my village to the Baptist mission school. There were 150 students at the school, all boys, from both Hindu and tribal families. Many of the them were day students, commuting from their nearby homes. The rest of us, mostly hill boys, stayed in one large dormitory, with several boys assigned to each room.

All the other boarding students went home during the summer and winter vacations, but I never had the money for the long trip home. I usually had to work hard during the month-and-a-half vacation in order to earn money to buy supplies for the next few months of schooling. I always looked for a job before the vacation began, but seldom found one that paid well. Every year I found it unpleasant when everyone left the dormitory, about 140 boys packed and gone. I was the only one left in the big dormitory. All alone at night, I would listen to the jackals howling at the moon. Then all would be silent.

During the second year of high school I decided that I was not going to stay alone that year. I had been at the school through one year and a half. I was determined to go home this vacation like everyone else. I worked hard, but as vacation approached, I wondered whether I would have enough money to get home.

The first rains of the approaching monsoon season had begun to fall high up in the mountains. The small mountain creeks carried the water down to the valley, emptying into the narrow Toklai River that flowed through the compound, dividing the high school and dormitory from the church and mission bungalow offices. The British Army had constructed a bridge over the river during World War II, when the school had been used to house Italian prisoners of war.

A sudden flash flood of spring rains had eroded the mountainsides, bringing a lot of uprooted bamboo trees and dead wood down from the mountains. A few larger trees had caught on the pilings of the bridge and now trapped all the smaller branches, vines and other debris that were flowing downstream. If the jam was not removed soon, the bridge was sure to give way.

Before classes began, the principal, Dr. J.W. Cook, called for volunteers to clear away the debris. But no one dared swim the river's swift currents, let alone remove the branches clogging the bridge. Even the best of swimmers could not be certain of his fate.

One thing was certain. The bridge was going to break loose from its foundation if something was not done right away. Rev. Longri Ao, the Bible teacher, offered twenty-five rupees to anyone who would do the task. This was my chance to earn cash for my trip home during summer vacation.

"I will do it," I offered.

I armed myself with a light axe, a knife and fifty feet of rope. I tied one end of the rope to a post near the bridge, and the other end around my waist. In case the current took me away, I would have a second chance.

As I waded into the cold, muddy water, I breathed a quick prayer. Fellow students watched from all sides. I swam out to the jam and started chopping. Four hours later I saw the last of the branches float downstream. The bridge was cleared. I shouted triumphantly as I untied myself and swam the half mile down to the dormitory. What a victorious swim that was!

The current was so swift that I didn't even need to paddle. The entire student body watched as I drifted down. As I came ashore, they cheered, and Rev. Ao greeted me.

"I knew, I knew you could do it!"

I had earned enough money to go home for vacation.

Two months later, I took a rickshaw to the train station, and hopped on the train. Two days later I transferred to a bus at Silchar. Finally I reached a little town called Lakhipur, which is on the Barak River. From here I had to travel by boat. The Barak River boats were not like the cruise ships on television! They were tiny country vessels, about fifteen feet long. In the middle of each boat was just enough room for one person to sleep underneath the matted bamboo canopy. As I wandered along the shore, I found a Bengali boatman my father had hired before.

The Bengali boatman stated his price, and I agreed. Two rupees per day. But when I told him I wanted to go upstream into the hill area, he refused.

"You see way up there, in the mountains, about a hundred miles away?" he asked. "There is a heavy thunderstorm there. We'd better wait five days until the storm is over and the flooding waters subside. The river will swell up and we will not be able to fight the current."

I was not about to waste five precious days of my vacation in Lakhipur. This was my first vacation home in a year and a half.

"No!" I retorted. "I only have a limited vacation. We are going."

"I know this river a lot better than you do. I grew up on this river. If I say we are not going, we are *not going!*"

"I have traveled a lot here, too. We can make it," I insisted. Still he refused, so I offered, "If we go today, I will help you row the boat. If we wait five days, you will have to row the boat by yourself."

Finally he gave in, but not without a last warning: "All right, we will start. But if we have any problems on the way, don't blame me."

We rowed the rest of that afternoon, camping on the shore at sunset. The next morning we could see the rains beginning to fall. As we rowed, the boatman began to get worried. I sang songs I had learned at Jorhat, trying to calm him down. That night, we camped by the river again.

The next morning, the river had swollen. The rains we had seen from Lakhipur pouring over the mountains had drained into the river. The current was now much swifter, and the Bengali boatman did not want to row.

"We will not go any more. We will stay right here until the river goes down."

"No," I said. "We must go on. I have to get home!"

"How can a small boat like mine go against that strong of a current? Impossible!"

"We will do it together. I will be on the front, and you on the back." After much encouragement, I finally persuaded him. He untied the boat and we began to row. The current was so strong that instead of going upstream, no matter how hard we rowed, we slipped downstream. The current was much faster and stronger than I had thought. We were swept downstream about a half-mile before we were able to get back to shore. The boatman was very angry with me.

"I told you! I told you we couldn't do it. We should have just stayed in my hometown and we wouldn't have to suffer this."

He tied the boat to the top of a tree that was now under ten feet of water. The river kept rising higher and higher. We had to untie and retie the rope three times because of the climbing water level. I couldn't believe that the river could reach that high, but the boatman had known it all along. We spent the whole day and night there, waiting for the water level to go down. The next morning the river was still too high, so we spent another day there. We were not even on shore. We were still on the boat tied to the top of a tree. There was no place to go. We spent another night sleeping in the hull of that little boat. The next morning, we awoke and still the water level had not gone down far enough. For breakfast we ate the last of our supplies. There was no village or town in sight. The boatman wanted to go back. But there was no way I would go back downstream.

"As soon as the river subsides, we will find a village where I can buy rice," I offered.

"The next village is quite far away. We *must* go back," he insisted.

"Don't worry," I told him, "God will supply our needs." I would not give in, so we spent that whole day without food or water. The river water was so muddy that we could not drink it. By the next morning, the fifth day of this ordeal, we were really hungry and tired of being stuck in one place. Somehow, the water was still not subsiding as much as it should have. But it had gone down some, so I was ready to go on.

"Look across to the other side," I said to the boatman. "The water is a lot calmer. Let's cross over and slowly go up."

"I know enough about the river," he protested. "It is not any easier on the other side."

"We are going to the other side because I know it's milder," I insisted. "We can do it together."

Finally, he relented. "All right! Untie it!"

I untied the boat and we tried to cross the river. At the middle of the river the current was so strong that we were swept another half mile downstream. I had never encountered such a strong current. Our muscles and all of our energy didn't amount to anything against that current. We were swept down and across the river. When we landed on the other side, I looked back across and once again saw how mild the river looked on the side we'd just come from.

The side we were now on was much worse. The current was just as strong, and there was no place to tie the boat. We eased the boat up the shoreline looking for a better place to stop and rest. Up ahead I saw a big rock. I figured that if we could get ahead of the rock, we could lodge ourselves between it and the shore. The boatman was willing to try, since we were in no position to stop and wait where we were.

As we tried to maneuver around the rock, we were hit by an even stronger current. Water was being forced around the rock, colliding with the other currents. This combined force tipped our boat hard on its side. I thought we had capsized, but the boat settled back to a level position. When I looked inside the boat, there was a *masheer*, a large river fish, flopping around in the shallow water in the boat.

The *masheer* is the tastiest of the Indian river fish. This one had to weigh at least twenty-five pounds. Forgetting about the swirling current, I jumped on the fish, putting my hand inside its mouth so it could not escape. I held on tightly to the fish until the Bengali boatman was able to tie the boat. He gave me a piece of rope and I withdrew my hand from the fish's mouth.

The Bengali cleaned the fish and cooked it over a small fire. That night we slept with full stomachs. The next morning we ate some more of the fish for break-fast. As we got back into the boat, the Bengali said, "The river has gone down. We can go on."

We rowed the boat together for two more days. I'll never forget when he dropped me on the shore at the end of the journey. He took my baggage out of the boat and carried it up the hill. As he set it down, he looked at me and said, "Your God must be big." Three times he said this to me.

I looked him back in the eye and said, "My God is *very* big. He owns the whole world, you and me."

Tears came down his face as he reached over and hugged me. No Bengali ever does that. He waved his hand at me as he got back into his boat. "Don't take another boatman for your future trips. I want to take you every time."

As I watched him floating downstream, I thought, "Yes, my God is big. He knew I needed to go home and see my parents. He provided a job so I could earn my fare. When I needed protection, He provided it even though my stubbornness had caused my predicament. When we needed food, He provided a huge *masheer*. My God supplied all my needs."

ANGRY
NAGA BOYS

• • • • • • •

I will not fear what man
shall do unto me.
Hebrews 13:6

During the first two years at Jorhat Christian High School, in order to pay for my room and board, I was in charge of sweeping the dormitory that housed 150 boys. World War II was just over, and military clothing was both plentiful and fashionable. So every student wore military boots. By evening, the dirt floors of the dormitory looked like a disaster area.

It was my duty every morning to bring water from a pond a half mile away and sprinkle it over the entire dirt floor. If there were any ruts or holes, I was to fill them in and smooth them over. For all that labor, I was given one-quarter of a rupee. That was less than two cents a day.

After my second year, the principal of the school, Dr. J.W. Cook, was so pleased with the job I was doing that he promoted me. The promotion put me in charge of the cleanliness of the entire compound. I didn't have any regular working hours, but I had to maintain the whole campus, working whenever I wanted or needed to. Dr. Cook was particularly concerned that the dining hall be cleaned regularly, because many students were suffering from dysentery. The filth in the dining area had attracted flies, which spread disease-causing germs.

Nevertheless, tribal boys are tribal boys. They would eat their meal of rice, *dhal* (a split-pea-like vegetable), and beef, lamb or pork curry. What was left over would usually end up on the floor. My first order of business was to demand that all unwashed plates be brought to one place so that the dishwasher could take care of them properly. But even this was not easy.

One of the boys at the high school was named Chuba; he was not yet a committed Christian. Chuba was from the Ao Naga tribe. He was a very good volleyball player and the star of our football team, but he was also short-tempered and a bully. When Chuba heard that I was in charge of the cleanliness of the dining hall, he smeared his leftover rice on the table and poured curry juice on it. Disease-carrying flies flocked to this mess.

For three days in a row I reminded him that he should heed the rules, but he continued to make messes. I told him that I had no choice but to report him to Dr. Cook. Chuba became enraged: "If you report me, I'll kill you. I'm stronger than you. If you do that, you will be dead."

I really didn't believe he would kill me, but I

decided to wait and see what would happen the next day. That evening, he did it again. I went to tell Dr. Cook, but unfortunately he was not in his bungalow. Chuba, however, heard that I had gone to report him.

That evening, during the study hour between seven and nine o'clock, all the Ao Naga boys disappeared from the study hall. I didn't understand why. When the study hour was over, I returned to my room in the dormitory. To the door of my room was attached a large cardboard with a crude drawing of a human skull and crossbones on one side and a huge knife on the other. Underneath was the inscription, *ROCHUNGA, TONIGHT YOUR HEAD WILL BE CUT OFF.* I stared at the sign and stood silently for a few moments. As I entered my room, I removed the poster and placed it under my bed. I knelt down to pray, "Lord, what shall I do? I fear they mean to do this. What shall I do, Lord?"

Apparently, many students passing by the room before I arrived had seen the sign; I could hear them congregating in the hall. There was a lot of anxious whispering among them. They knew that the Ao Naga boys were only a generation removed from headhunters.

The tribal students from my home state of Manipur came to my room and said we would have to defend ourselves with our own weapons, for we could not be intimidated. They called an emergency meeting to discuss how we would fight the gang of Naga boys. Soon they had determined that *now* was the time to fight. Within a few minutes everyone brought whatever weapon he had to fight with –

sticks, stones and knives. I told them, "These boys will not chop my head off. If we fight them now, we will only create trouble and violence on the campus. Don't worry about me!"

But the eight boys from Manipur stayed in my room until midnight. All the Naga boys were absent from the dormitory, so two of the boys went out to spy where the Nagas were gathered. They discovered that beyond the high school building the Naga boys were having a secret meeting and were armed with large, headhunting knives. They were definitely planning something.

The two spies came back reporting what they had seen. "We *must* fight," they insisted.

I said, "No, there are about fifty Naga boys, and there are only a few of us. What chance would we have? No, we must not fight. I will take care of it myself."

At about two in the morning, I persuaded my friends to return to their rooms. Before I lay down, I went to the door to lock it, but found that the lock was broken. Two of my roommates – Naga boys – were absent. Another was a Garo, and he had decided to move out for the night. Only one freshman student, Lotha, was in the room. He was a Naga, but had not associated with the others.

I knelt down beside my bed to read by the flickering candlelight. I opened my Bible and read portions from Philippians and Hebrews 13:5-6: "I will never leave thee, nor forsake thee. So that we may boldly say, The Lord is my helper, and I will not fear what man shall do unto me."

I said to myself, "If God cannot help me, no one else can." With this consolation, I committed my life into the Lord's hands. I prayed, "Lord, if they are going to cut off my head, let them do it swiftly and completely. Don't let them just seriously wound me. If you are going to preserve me, then please give me sleep."

I crawled into bed and in seconds I was sleeping deeply. The next morning, I awoke while it was still dark, but there was enough light to see my freshman roommate sitting on the floor, leaning against the door. "Lotha," I exclaimed. "What are you doing?"

"After you went to bed I decided to watch out for you. I have been sitting here all night."

"Did anything happen?"

"I heard them come up to the door many times, and I thought something was going to happen, but they always went away."

I was touched by Lotha's loyalty. "Lotha, before I went to bed, I read this Bible verse, 'The Lord is my helper. I will not fear what man shall do unto me.' I wish I had told you this, so you wouldn't have had to sit all night against the door."

I didn't tell Dr. Cook about the incident, but the next morning he knew there had been a disturbance in the dormitory. He came to me and offered me a room in his bungalow.

"No," I said. "I was here all night and I was safe."

I will never forget Dr. Cook's prayer that morning. He poured out his heart to God that the work of the devil should be suppressed and destroyed, and that the love of Christ should triumph at Jorhat

Christian High School. He called the Naga boys over and prayed with the leaders. His prayer of love for them was one I thought only God could utter.

Dr. Cook was a great man of God and a firm disciplinarian. I was sure he would punish the gang leaders, but I was worried about what would happen to them if they were expelled from the school. They would have to return to their villages. What would become of them?

Two days later, as I was walking to attend the evening prayer meeting, one of the leaders of the Nagas – Maren – came up behind me. He grabbed my arm and hugged me. Before I could say a word, he cried. He asked for my forgiveness. I readily forgave him and told him I felt no hatred against him. With tears in our eyes, we walked into the prayer meeting together.

At the close of the meeting Chuba and two other leaders came to me. They confessed they had gone to my room several times, intending to cut off my head, but something had stopped them. One of them kissed me on the neck, and another on the cheek. They all wept and asked for forgiveness. Chuba was sincerely repentant as he sobbed, "I am so sorry."

I was very impressed with the changed attitudes of my former enemies, and my heart was filled with love for them. This demonstration of "the power of His resurrection" (Phil 3:10) made me very much aware of God's presence and protection in my life.

A few months later I went to Makokchung, the capital town of the Ao Nagas to attend the Naga Student Union Conference as an observer. I was very warmly received and asked to speak to the entire assembly. As I traveled from one village to another, I found the Nagas are the most hospitable people. I was invited to eat in three or four homes every day. Some of my closest friends in high school and university were Naga students. They are simple, truthful and trustworthy.

TIBETAN
BIBLE

• • • • • •

To obey is better than sacrifice.
1 Samuel 15:22

In 1949, I began my studies at St. Paul's College, under the University of Calcutta. Leaving the hills of northeastern India for Calcutta was quite a large step for me. Most people of my tribe had never traveled more than a hundred miles from their birthplace. Yet here I was, studying at a huge university in a city of millions of people, eight hundred miles from my home. Often I would wonder in amazement at how far God had brought me as I pursued my goal to translate the Bible into the Hmar language.

I found good fellowship with other believers at the Carey Baptist Church, a church that had been founded many years before by William Carey, the father of the modern missionary movement. The pastor was Walter Corlett, a magnificent musician and preacher, and a man who truly loved God and the people of India. He seldom invited guest speakers for Sunday morning services, but on Sunday evenings he often had special speakers, which were always a blessing to us students.

On one particular Sunday evening, a missionary lady was invited to speak. Mrs. H.C. Bowker had come to India as a missionary and married a Christian businessman in Calcutta. Her husband was the president of the Calcutta Electric Works, the company that supplied the electricity for the entire city of Calcutta. After she married, Mrs. Bowker had continued her missionary work.

Mrs. Bowker was at our church to represent the Bible Society's special need to print a Bible in the Tibetan language. She told us the story of the Tibetan Bible: Before World War II, a group of Indian Christians had been burdened and concerned that the Tibetans have a Bible in their own language. Some lay people had begun the translation work. When other scholars reviewed the manuscript, however, they felt it was not good enough. God laid upon the heart of Bishop Chandu Ray, the Bible Society's secretary, to oversee the translation of the Tibetan Bible.

Bishop Chandu Ray had become a Christian through the reading of the Bible. He had left his high-caste Hindu Brahmin family to pursue his love of the Word of God. One day Bishop Ray was praying about the Tibetan Bible and the need for a scholar to produce a good translation. God spoke to him, and he felt led to go to find a translator. He was led of the Holy Spirit to go to Kashmir.

Under the bridge near Srinagar in Kashmir, Mrs. Bowker told us, Bishop Ray found a Tibetan scholar by the name of Gargan. This man had gone through the most rigorous scholastic and metaphysical training at a Buddhist monastery in Tibet. One day Gargan had picked up a Bible and through his reading it he had become a follower of the Lord Jesus Christ. As a result, he had been excommunicated from the monastery by his fellow monks. When Bishop Ray found Gargan, he was tending a flock of sheep and living under a bridge. A scholar under a bridge!

Bishop Chandu Ray and Gargan began translating the Tibetan Bible, from the Gospel of Matthew through Revelation. When they had finished the New Testament, they soon found that there was no possible way to have the manuscript typeset in India. The handwritten manuscript would have to be photographed page by page. Gargan carefully rewrote the entire New Testament, using black India ink so it could be photographed.

Just as he finished, World War II broke out. The manuscript was sent to England. Before the Bible Society was able to photograph the manuscripts, the Germans began to bomb London. Fearing that the manuscript might be lost during the bombing, a Bible Society member took it outside of London and buried it someplace in the country. When the war was over, the manuscript was sent back to India to be printed. But there had been a delay in manufacturing the Bibles, due to lack of funds.

Mrs. Bowker gave a remarkable presentation of the need for the Tibetan Bible printing. I have never heard anyone speak more deeply about the need for Bibles in Bibleless societies. I was enthralled and challenged. It touched my heart, because my own people had been crying for the Bible to be translated into our own language. The Tibetans, too, had been waiting so long for the Bible. Now the manuscript was ready for print. Somehow, Mrs. Bowker's message hit the tender chords in me.

After Mrs. Bowker had finished, Dr. Walter Corlett came to the platform and said, "We would like to give from this church the most generous offering we have ever given. I'm praying that Mrs. Bowker will not have to go to another church before the Tibetan Bible will be given to the press. We are going to take an offering. Give generously."

On that evening I had brought with me five students from my dormitory. I had promised them that I would pay for their streetcar fare if they would come with me to church. I had just received my scholarship money and my wallet was in good shape, so I didn't mind paying for friends to come to church. I had paid for my tuition for the rest of the year, but not for my room and board. I thought I would pay that on Monday.

As they passed the offering plates, there was a tug of war between my heart and my head. My heart was saying, "Give everything you've got. Empty everything into the offering plate."

My head was saying, "Just give ten bucks. Be reasonable." The tug of war was quite intense as my heart and my head began to argue with each other. My head continued, "If you give everything you've got, what are you going to eat tomorrow? You haven't paid for your room and board; how will you continue your studies?"

My heart responded, "Give everything. Trust God." The struggle was so intense that I didn't even see the offering plate pass. It slipped right by.

As the meeting was coming to a close, Pastor Corlett offered a prayer of thanksgiving. He said, "I am going to do something that I have never done before. I honestly meant what I said about Mrs. Bowker not going to another church for money for the Tibetan Bible printing. Just in case there is someone who has not given, or someone who would like to give more, I'm going to leave a basket at the door. Pray as you leave the church, and if the Lord prompts you to give, give generously." My heart had won the battle by this time. I walked out and emptied all my money into the basket . . . enough money to pay for three months of room and board.

All my friends hopped on the bus; but I walked the five miles back to the dormitory. It was the most beautiful walk I have ever taken. I was so happy. When I reached the college, I saw that the gate had just been shut. It was very difficult to scale over the gate at St. Paul's College. Students were not supposed to be out that late, but I couldn't help it. I hadn't had money to pay for a bus ride. Fortunately, the *darwan* (gatekeeper) was very kind and came out from his little room to open the gate for me.

That night I realized that for the first time, I had given all the money I had for the Lord's work. I began to see the joy of giving in a way that I had never seen in all my life.

The next morning I got up praising the Lord. I didn't have anything except Jesus. If I needed anything, God would provide. I was so happy that God had enabled me to put that kind of faith in Him. He had brought me to Calcutta; now He would take care of me.

I went to the morning prayer meeting at seven o'clock. We finished the prayer and as I came out, the *darwan* who had opened the gate for me the night before handed me a white envelope bearing one word: "Rochunga." Inside there was a one hundred rupee bill. No letter, no message. Not even a signature. God met my need!

From that moment on, I never worried again for my own personal needs. Every time there has been a need, God has provided abundantly. My life verse, *He that speared not His own son but delivered Him up for us all, how shall He not with Him also freely give us all things* (Romans 8:32), became even more powerful.

To this day, the sight of a Tibetan Bible always brings to me immeasurable satisfaction. It reminds me of that moment when I discovered for myself the truth of the verse that says, "To obey is better than sacrifice."

PINEAPPLES
ON THE
TARMAC
· · · · · · ·

Every man is tempted, when he is
drawn away of his own lust, and enticed.
James 1:14

After I finished my second year of college training in
Calcutta, I was still tempted to be involved in some
form of business or another. Business had always
attracted me, and, of course, I wanted to make
money and help my people. I had seen what wealth
was all about in the big city of Calcutta. I thought I
could make a little myself. I had learned about making money during World War II and the desire to do
it had never left me. But my original calling was to
prepare myself to translate the Bible into the language of my people and I was not supposed to be
involved in any activities that would distract me
from that commitment until the job was done. I soon
learned my lesson the hard way.

I knew exactly what I was going to do to make lots of money. In Lakhipur, only eighteen miles from the Silchar airport, there was a place where I could buy a hundred pineapples for ten rupees, about two dollars. In Calcutta, I could sell them for two hundred rupees. That was not even at retail, but at wholesale price. I figured out my profits and decided to charter an airplane to take the pineapples to Calcutta. I went to a private airline called Sky Players and they willingly signed a contract with me. Though the cost of chartering the plane was three times as much as the cost of the pineapples in Lakhipur, I was still going to make a good profit.

My plan was to take these pineapples and transport them within a few hours from Silchar to Calcutta. Pineapples are highly perishable, so time was of the essence. I made the connection with a wealthy Calcutta fresh-fruit wholesale merchant, a Muslim named Ghulam Mohammad Rasul. He said, "I will buy as many pineapples as you can ship to Calcutta."

Arrangements were made that the airline crew, immediately upon arrival in Calcutta, would telephone Mr. Rasul. Mr. Rasul would then pick up the pineapples from Dum Dum Airport. An airplane load of pineapples was to be shipped at least three times a week, but not on Saturday or Sunday. I was to fly with the load of pineapples only every other week, in order to collect my money. When all the arrangements had been made in Calcutta, I returned to Lakhipur and arranged to take the pineapples from the farmers on consignment. They were so excited that I had found a ready market for their pineapples. There was no limit to the amount of pineapples they could provide me.

One week later, the first airplane arrived in Silchar. I loaded five thousand pineapples on it. The Cachar District is in the valley and is very hot. It was at least ninety-five degrees that day and very humid. I didn't mind, because something good was coming. The airplane taxied down the runway and took off. I waved good-bye to the pilot, and I began to count my eggs before they were even laid.

The next day, the plane came back. I loaded it up again and sent it on its way. The third day, the plane returned and once again I loaded it and waved good-bye. I began eagerly to count how much money I was going to have. I sent a telegram to Mr. Rasul, saying that I would be coming the next week. I asked him how things were going. To my great surprise, I received a telegram the next day.

PINEAPPLES HAVE NOT ARRIVED.

I couldn't believe it.

The plane did not come the next day because the weather was bad. I sent another telegram to Mr. Rasul.

THREE PLANE LOADS SHIPPED. PICK THEM UP AT AIRPORT. I WILL COME NEXT WEEK.

The next day, the cable reply came.

PINEAPPLES HAVE NOT ARRIVED.

I was shocked. I went to the airport, but for some reason, the charter plane had not arrived. I waited all day, but still the plane did not come. It now had been six days since I had sent the first planeload of pineapples.

The next day was Sunday. Since I had long before made a covenant not to work on Sunday, I did not go to the airport until Monday. When I reached the airport, the aircraft was not there. I was becoming very nervous. "What in the world is going on in Calcutta?" I wondered.

On Tuesday I went back to the airport with several truckloads of pineapples. I was sure that the plane would be there that day. The airplane finally arrived, and I loaded it up. I decided that I had to go down to Calcutta to see what was happening, and to pick up my money. I jumped into the plane and we flew to Calcutta.

When we landed at Dum Dum Airport, I couldn't believe my eyes. My three airplane loads of pineapples were piled all over the tarmac. The airline people had simply thrown the bamboo baskets on top of one another from the airplane. Most of the pineapples were crushed from the weight of the others piled on top. The juice was flowing all over the tarmac and the heat had made the juice into a sticky mess. The airport coolies were helping themselves to the few undamaged pineapples. I stood there for a long time in silence, while they unloaded the plane I had brought.

After the plane was unloaded, I hopped into a taxi and went to Mr. Rasul's office. "What in the world happened to you that you didn't come to the airport to pick up the pineapples?" I demanded.

Calmly, Mr. Rasul replied, "I was never telephoned or informed of their arrival."

"Hop in the cab with me and we will go over to the airport."

The Bengali Muslims exaggerate a little more than we tribal people. When Mr. Rasul saw the pineapple juice flowing all over the airport, he exclaimed, "*Babaree-ba!* I can almost swim in the juice!" Whether or not he seriously felt sorry for me, tears came flowing from the eyes of Mr. Rasul. He broke down and wept. "Why do they do things like this? Everyday I have been waiting for a call so I could pick them up and market them. Somebody has ruined us!"

By this time it was already late in the evening. There was nothing that we could do to salvage our produce. A friend of mine, Mr. Lal Rema, was staying at St. Paul's College dormitory while studying for his MA at the Calcutta University, so I went to his room to spend the night. Knowing that my dreams of wealth were flowing freely away on the tarmac, I couldn't sleep very well.

The next morning I returned to the airport with Mr. Rasul in his truck. He took his pick of the pineapples, mainly the fresh ones I had brought the day before, and loaded them onto his truck. After he paid me for those, I asked him, "How about the rest of them," pointing to the rotting mess.

"Well, sir," Mr. Rasul replied, "I can't market bad pineapples like those. There is nothing I can do." He continued, "You know pineapples don't last two days in the sun, and there is no market for damaged fruit. Look at the ones on top. They have been sitting there at least three or four days in the sun. When they have dark spots like those, no one will buy them." He drove away, leaving me standing on the tarmac with all the bad pineapples. I took off my shirt and began to open the pineapple crates. There were a few that were still good, so I separated these from the damaged ones. It took me almost the whole day.

The next day, I came back to the airport to find that all the good ones I had separated had been stolen. I was heartbroken again. I went through the pile of bad pineapples, and pulled out any that were not too badly damaged. These few I sold at the airport. I still had a huge pile of rotting pineapples. I called some of the coolies and beggars over. I told them to help themselves. I couldn't believe how fast the pile was gone.

I returned to Lal Rema's room and sat for a long time, brooding over my misfortune. How would I pay the people in Lakhipur for their pineapples? How was I going to pay for the chartered plane? The money Mr. Rasul had given me was not going to cover my expenses. But business is business. You have to settle all your accounts.

The next day I went to the airlines office and met the general manager. I explained to him how they had literally bankrupted me. He listened to my story very patiently.

"I don't understand why it happened, but I must admit it was our fault," he replied. "I see very clearly here in the consignment notices that we were to inform Mr. Rasul when the pineapples arrived. Obviously we didn't do that."

After a moment's thought he offered, "Under the circumstances, I have no reason to ask you to pay. I have to accept the loss on our part." I was relieved. That took some of the sting away from the misfortune. But still, I had to face my own people in Lakhipur without money to pay them. What was I going to do?

Instead of flying to Silchar, I flew to Imphal, Manipur. In those days, the tribal people wove most of their own clothes with cotton yarn they had either grown themselves or bought in the city. For some reason, there was a great scarcity of cotton yarn in the Lakhipur area. I knew that there was an abundant supply in Manipur, only thirty-five minutes away by plane. The only problem was that special permission was needed to export cotton yarn from Manipur and only the Deputy Commissioner had the authority to grant the export permit.

Upon arrival in Imphal, I was pleased to learn that an old friend of mine, Mr. M.N. Phukan, was now the Deputy Commissioner of Manipur. When he had first traveled across the hills of Manipur, as a Commissioner, he had needed an interpreter. I had been called to travel and interpret for him, so I knew him well. I went directly to Mr. Phukan's house and told him of my plight.

"Sir, I need your help," I began. "I don't like asking for favors, but this one time I must ask you. I would like to buy as much cotton yarn as I can with the little money I have with me and take it to Silchar and Lakhipur. Could you please give me a written permit?" I pleaded.

"How many bundles of cotton yarn do you want to take?" he asked.

"Well, I could take a lot, but I don't have the money. I want to buy as much as I can afford." I counted my money and told him the amount.

"Come to my office tomorrow morning at 10 a.m. and your need will be cared for."

I was delighted. The next morning I went to Mr. Phukan's office and he handed me a piece of paper. I read it. "Permission granted for Rochunga Pudaite to transport from Manipur to Silchar as much yarn as he can carry in one trip." I thanked Mr. Phukan repeatedly for his favor.

As I walked out of his office, I held the paper in both hands and kissed it. It was a miracle. I went down to the market and bargained for as much cotton yarn as I could buy with the money I had, saving enough to buy an airplane ticket and some spending money. I bargained hard with the merchants, finally reaching an agreement. In those days, there were no taxis in Imphal, so I hired several rickshaws, piled them high with the cotton yarn, and headed for the airport.

When I reached Silchar, everybody was amazed at the amount of yarn I had with me. Everyone wanted to buy the yarn. I went first to the people to whom

I owed money for the pineapples. All of them said they would rather be paid with the yarn than with cash. I made deals with the farmers so that the payment of yarn would cover my debt to each of them. Often, the yarn wasn't quite sufficient to cover the debt, but when they heard my story, they were willing to settle for my offer.

After I had taken care of all the business, I took a small country boat up the Barak River to my parents' village. While I had been involved in the pineapple business, I had not read my Bible once. I had been too busy to read. As I lay in the hull of the boat, I opened my Bible and began to read, "If any of you lack wisdom, let him ask of God, that giveth to all men liberally, and upbraideth not." (James 1:5) I was blessed. I lacked wisdom, but I had God's promise.

The word *upbraideth* in the English language is a little difficult to understand, but in the Lushai translation, it is much simpler. There it is translated "scold". God gives wisdom without scolding. All He asks is that we "ask in faith, nothing wavering. For he that wavereth is like a wave of the sea driven with the wind and tossed. For let not that man think that he shall receive any thing of the Lord." (James 1:6-7)

I continued reading. These words really hit me hard: "A double minded man is unstable in all his ways." (James 1:8) I wanted to do the will of God and translate the Bible into the Hmar language and preach the Word of God. But I also had the desire to make money and get rich and drive a beautiful red

Hilman Mink car, and live in a beautiful home like those of the rich Hindus and Muslims I saw in Calcutta.

The words of the Bible slowly sank into my thick skull. "Every man is tempted, when he is drawn away of his own lust, and enticed." (James 1:14) I had been drawn away from my studies and translation work, and had been enticed by the promises of this world. Inside that little boat, I really had a session with God. I promised Him that I would seek His guidance in everything.

I reached home four days later. I told my parents of my escapade. After listening to my story, my father said, "Son, I'm glad you came home alive. Go back to school. We are still waiting for you to translate the Bible." Sitting with my parents on the porch, I recommitted my life to the "Father of lights, with whom is no variableness, neither shadow of turning." (James 1:17)

A VERY
PRESENT HELP
• • • • • • •

*This I recall to my mind, therefore have I
hope.
It is of the Lord's mercies that we are not
consumed,
because His compassions fail not.
They are new every morning:
Great is Thy faithfulness.
Lamentations 3:21-23*

After graduating from St. Paul's College I enrolled
in Allahabad University, located in Allahabad, a
large city in northern India. During my first year at
the university, my Christian faith and fervent desire
to witness caused a lot of conflicts with my fellow
students. I spent a great deal of time debating the
merits of Christianity against the beliefs of
Hinduism and Islam. I had always thought that
Christianity was the truth, but had never been really

challenged. Now, at the university, I was put to the test daily by some of the best thinkers of India, both professors and students.

In January of 1953 I began to have pains in my lower abdomen. I went to the school infirmary to see a doctor. After examining me, the physician advised me to have my appendix removed. It had become inflamed and, though not very serious yet, it was in danger of becoming far worse if it were not treated.

"I can't go to the hospital," I argued with the doctor. "I don't have the money to pay for the bill."

"Well," the doctor replied. "I'll give you this medicine, but if the inflammation doesn't subside, you must go to the hospital." The doctor was insistent, but since he hadn't taken an x-ray, I didn't believe him.

I bought the medicine he had prescribed, but I determined that I would not go to the hospital, even if the pain did not go away. This was one week I could not afford to be laid up in a hospital, because in just a few days Dr. Bob Pierce, an American evangelist whom I had met the previous year in Calcutta, was coming to Allahabad to speak at a Youth For Christ rally. As one of the local leaders of Youth For Christ, I wanted to be on the platform with that great man of God.

At a meeting to organize the rally, Youth For Christ director Major Cyril Thompson told us, "We have to do everything we can to get the largest possible crowd for this great American evangelist." He wanted all the Christian students to put posters on billboards and to give out handbills on the street to passersby.

I was so happy. I determined that if a great Christian like Bob Pierce was coming to Allahabad, I definitely wasn't going to be sitting on the sidelines. After all, I had been constantly bombarded with the teachings of Hinduism, Islam and other religions, clashing with many of my fellow students in head-on collisions. I thought that if I brought these skeptics to hear Bob Pierce, someone so much more eloquent than I, perhaps they would be more receptive to my own witnessing.

By Friday morning, however, my stomachache became so severe that I knew I would not be able to participate in the rally. I went to Cyril Thompson's house to tell him how very disappointed I was that I would not be able to hang any more posters because of the pain.

To my great surprise, Dr. Bob Pierce was having breakfast with the Thompsons. Major Thompson made the introductions. Instead of a polite handshake, the renowned evangelist gave me a big bear hug and said, "How are you, buddy?" I told him I was fine. I didn't say anything about my appendix problem. We chatted briefly. I was impressed by the warmth of his personality.

As I was leaving, he gave me another hug and slipped some money into my coat pocket. I didn't look in my pocket until I returned to the dormitory. I expected to find a few rupees, the equivalent perhaps of a dollar or two, but it was 150 rupees. In those days one dollar was equivalent to almost five rupees.

That night, as I lay in bed trying to sleep, the pain

became intolerable. I was sure that it was because I had bicycled to the rally. Unable to sleep, I began to weigh my options. I did not want to be operated on in a government hospital. I remembered the 150 rupees that Dr. Bob had given me. I could use that money to go to a Christian hospital in Kachhwa, about three hours away by train from Allahabad. The chief medical officer of that hospital, Dr. Quinten Everard, was a fine Christian surgeon from Ireland. I had heard him speak at one of our Youth For Christ meetings, and had been very blessed.

Without even writing or telephoning the hospital, the next morning I took the train to Kachhwa. It was early in the morning and I didn't even have a friend to take me to the train station. I was in considerable pain by the time the train pulled into the Kachhwa station. I asked the conductor how far it was to the hospital. To my dismay it was still a mile and a half away.

I started to walk in the direction he had pointed, but the pain was so great that I knew I wouldn't make it. As I was standing by the side of the road, resting from the pain, a two-wheeled cart pulled by two large bulls passed by. I stopped the driver and said, "Driver, take me to the mission hospital. I'll give you some rupees." I was in so much pain that I don't remember how much I offered him.

Slowly the bullock cart took me to the hospital. The wooden wheels seemed to magnify every little bump in the road. We finally arrived. After paying and thanking the driver, I asked the first nurse I could find to take me to Dr. Everard. She took me to his office right away.

Dr. Everard asked me my name. I told him, and he said, "I heard your testimony at the Oriental Mission Society in Allahabad. I was very blessed. What can I do for you?"

Putting my hand on my right side, I said, "Something is troubling me here. I can hardly sit or stand." It didn't take very long for him to diagnose the problem.

"I see you have an appendix that needs to be taken out. I'll arrange for surgery." Soon I was in the surgery room, lying on the operating table. As they administered the anesthesia, Dr. Everard laid his hands on my forehead. The nurse held my feet, and two others held my hands. Then Dr. Everard prayed to God for guidance as he performed the surgery. I fell unconscious before their prayer was finished, but I felt such comfort hearing that man of God pray. I knew that I was in good hands.

The next thing I knew, I was waking up in a hospital room with five or six other patients. Dr. Everard asked if I would like to take a room in the mission bungalow. I was honored that he asked me, and agreed to it. The orderlies carried me over to the bungalow and settled me into a private room. Dr. Everard came over to my bed and said, "Do you know how close you were to having a rupture? If you had waited another day, I would not have been able to save you. In tropical weather like this, you would have been gone. You came just in the nick of time." All I could do was praise the Lord for His faithfulness.

I returned to Allahabad, and I was happy to learn that Dr. Bob Pierce was still in India. I went to him and said, "Dr. Bob, if it had not been for the Lord's mercy, I would not be here. My appendix would have ruptured and killed me. Your gift saved my life."

How good God is. He works through people who make themselves available to Him.

KUMBH MELA

• • • • • • •

But when He saw the multitudes, He was
moved with compassion on them,
because they fainted, and were
scattered abroad, as sheep having
no shepherd.
Matthew 9:36

Soon after I arrived in Allahabad, I became very
much aware of the strength of Hinduism and its
deep-rooted hold upon our Indian society. I also realized that Allahabad means "the Abode of Allah." On
one side of the city is a huge Muslim mosque, and on
the opposite side stands a large Hindu temple. The
University of Allahabad I attended and the dormitory in which I stayed were sandwiched between these
two great religious structures.

One day I went to the Sangam, a suburb of
Allahabad, where the rivers Ganges and Jumna come
together. Hindus believe at the convergence of the
two rivers an invisible goddess lies dormant. Once

every seven years, at a certain eclipse of a certain star, the goddess of the river floats to the surface, they believe. If you take a dip in the water while the goddess is on the surface, all your guilt is removed. Normally the goddess will "appear" at dawn and remain on the surface until the sun is above the horizon, approximately for two hours after sunrise.

The year I was in Allahabad was the particular year the goddess was to surface. It was February 1953, and three million Hindus from all over India converged at Sangam to dip in the water of the Ganges. The occasion is called Kumbh Mela. Even the president and prime minister of India came to take part in the Mela.

I had volunteered to serve in the crowd-control unit. Since all the Hindus wanted to be in the water, many in the crowd-control teams were Christians. I had never before seen three million people in one place. Many had camped together by the water for weeks without proper toilet facilities, all waiting for the great event to take place. There was a big mound along the river that everyone had to climb in order to go down to the river. The mound had been built to stop floods. From there we controlled the crowd, with ropes pulled tightly across the mound. People were to take their dip and walk out on both sides of the shoreline. It was quite a sight, three million anxious and weary pilgrims waiting for the right moment.

It reminded me of the story told in the Gospel of John where Jesus met the paralyzed man who was waiting by the pool in Bethesda. When an angel moved the water, the first person who entered the pool was healed of his disease. But the paralyzed man had no one to help him get into the water.

A similar expectancy and helplessness existed among these Hindus. They hoped that a dip in the Ganges River would help them recover from their diseases and spiritual sicknesses.

Hindu *fakirs* were everywhere. *Fakirs* are religious zealots who wear no clothes and throw ashes on themselves. Some put spikes through their tongues with a promise never to speak again until they can be completely free from telling lies. Some stood in the branches of trees on only one leg, hoping that this would bring them salvation. Many brought their beds of thorns to lie on. Some walked on burning coal. I tried to witness the gospel to some of these people, but they were so intent on the cleansing dip that they did not listen.

Finally the day came. At dawn, the temple priest blew a big conch, signifying the start of the dipping. The first group went down to take their dip in the Ganges. The water was absolutely filthy from all the wastes of three million people, but they all jumped in with great enthusiasm. The sun came up and nearly half of the crowd still waited for their chance. By about eight-thirty, they began to notice that the sun was rising rapidly; they realized the chances were slim of their getting into the water before it was too late. People began to push their way to the front. It was impossible to control the crowd. In their frenzy they rolled over the mound and stampeded.

I looked down from the mound at the people running all over, stepping on one another and jumping into the water. People were falling like flies, many never to rise again. Behind the crowd in the water laid an uncounted number of bodies. It was pathetic.

It was a miracle that I was not one of those who were trampled, because I was on the mound trying to direct the crowd where the biggest stampede took place. I came out alive only by the grace of God.

By noon we had picked up more than four hundred dead bodies and loaded them onto trucks. They were transported to a huge warehouse, where they were stacked up, waiting to be claimed by relatives and loved ones. For any thoughtful person, whether Christian, Muslim or Hindu, there is no way to fully understand the impact of such an event. I was exhausted after the last body was loaded. I prayed, "Lord, is there any hope for life? Is there any hope for human beings?"

I returned to the tea hut where I had left my bicycle that morning and cycled back to the dormitory. All the way I just shook by head, saying, "Lord, is there any hope in this world?" When I got back to my room, I picked up the devotional book I had read that morning and turned to the Bible text: It was from John 3, where the Lord Jesus said, "God so loved the world, that He gave His only begotten Son, that whosoever believeth in Him should not perish, but have everlasting life." The words I had read so many times came alive to me.

Yes, there is hope. There is hope in Jesus Christ. There is eternal life, God's gift to mankind.

THE
LOST PEN
• • • • • • •

The Son of Man is come to seek
and to save that which was lost.
Luke 19:10

At Allahabad University I enrolled in a course enti-
tled "Comparative Studies in Religion." I had a fine
professor, Mr. Kaul, an Oxford-educated Kashmiri
Brahmin. He was the author of several books on philosophy, and was the head of the philosophy department.

As Mr. Kaul lectured one day, he wrote on the
chalkboard the great religions of the world, and com-
pared their different approaches to God. He showed
the Hindus' seeking God through self-denial, the
Muslims' struggle to find Allah through doing good
works, and the Buddhists' search for the tranquility
of the soul – not for a god-being. He then described
the Christians' understanding of man away from
God, and God searching for man. He commented
that this was the most unbelievable, "topsy-turvy

religion," in which God would "wait for man to come to him." He said that if God is so big and mighty and great, why should he be searching and looking for man, who is so puny and insignificant, like a drop of water in the ocean.

Professor Kaul claimed that he had read the whole Bible, from Genesis to Revelation, and was certain that Christianity lets God search for man. He ridiculed this belief, then he went on to describe the great Hindu religious leaders and teachers; their search for God was very intense, he said. Many left everything in the world hoping to find peace and bliss. Yet, despite all their efforts and sacrifices, they ended up not finding God.

I raised my hand and said, "Sir, I don't have the whole answer, but I don't want to accept what you said about Christianity. I don't want you to say that it is an impossible religion. If it is an impossible religion, then there is no way that people should follow Christ. Right now I don't have an answer for you, but I won't accept that Christianity is impossible."

Before I came back to the class the next day, I did everything I could to prepare myself to debate the professor. But I soon discovered that I was powerless to stand up against the man's knowledge, eloquence, logic and sarcasm. For every argument I offered, he countered with another argument that made Christianity look utterly ridiculous.

All the while, I kept thinking of those Hindus who had gone down to the Ganges River for a holy dip in the muddy water. They were so helpless. Many had died. I had talked to many Hindus after they had taken a dip in the Ganges. They did not feel a sense of regeneration. In fact, many of my own classmates who had taken the dip told me they did not feel any internal change. Not one I talked to felt any better. These two experiences – the classroom teaching and the Kumbh Mela – created a great spiritual battle and hunger in me. After two months of Mr. Kaul's religion class, I was about to admit to myself, "Maybe *my* Christianity is an impossible, ridiculous religion."

One evening a friend of mine, Chiten Jamir, challenged me to a badminton game. I have always enjoyed sports, especially soccer and javelin. I accepted his challenge and we had a great game. I came home wet with perspiration, and took a shower. Later when I took out my books to begin working on my lessons, I realized that my pen was not with my books. It was the first good pen I had ever bought. I had used it for three years. I had carved my initials on it. I looked all over my room for it. It was already dark, but I went outside looking for it on the campus.

Early the next morning I woke up and searched for it again. Finally I concluded that one of the servants in the dormitory must have stolen it. I called the servants and harshly scolded them. They swore they had not taken it.

Twice a day a certain fellow came around the dormitory selling edible treats to the students. I thought he might have gone into my room and stolen my pen. I confronted him, but he also swore he hadn't taken it.

"If I did things like that, I wouldn't have a business," he declared. I believed him. For a whole week I missed my pen.

One afternoon the thought came to me that when Chiten Jamir had challenged me to the badminton game, I had so readily accepted that I hadn't even taken the time to change my shirt. My pen must still have been in my pocket when we started the game. I went down to the badminton court and looked around. Many people had played since our match. I thought there would be no chance of finding my pen. But I kept looking anyway.

I was about to leave the court when another thought came to me. At one point in the game, one of the fellows had hit the birdie into the brush. I had retrieved it, and my pen might have slipped out and still be there. I went to the bushes, leaned over, and there was a pen. I picked it up and turned it over slowly in my hand. My initials were there! I ran back to my room, thanking God that I had found my lost pen.

That night as I was sitting alone in my room, I read the story of Jesus' encounter with Zacchaeus. I came across the beautiful verses of Luke 19:9-10, where Jesus says to Zacchaeus, "This day is salvation come to this house forsomuch as he also is a son of Abraham. For the Son of Man is come to seek and to save that which was lost." If God had not sought after us, we would never have the capacity to find Him. All seeking would have been in vain.

In the same way, my best pen had no way of standing up on its own and saying, "Ro, I am lost. I am trying to find you." It couldn't shout to me. If it could have shouted, I'm sure it would have. It was I who had bought it and carved my initials on it. I, the owner, had to go all over the campus looking for that pen until I found it.

I turned to the Book of Genesis. "In the beginning *God* . . ."! I hadn't begun it. It began with God. God created man in His own image. God carved His initials on us. That's why God is looking for man. The Creator is Master of the created.

All of a sudden I began drawing a new diagram: God seeking for man. Man had no way of seeking for God. Man would have no way of finding Him if God had not revealed Himself in the person of Jesus Christ. Even after man had been created in God's own image, God had to pay for the penalty of our sin. The pen had been made, but I had to buy that pen and carve my initials on it. Likewise, I am bought with a price, the blood of the Son of God. God put His initial on me.

From that time on Christianity made a lot more sense to me. It was no longer just a religion to me. I understood that Christ had given His own life on my behalf so that I could have a way back into the presence of God through Him.

The next day in my religion class I explained my discovery to Professor Kaul and the other students. Professor Kaul was surprised at the wisdom of my discovery, and he was even touched by this new understanding. Never again did he make fun of me for my Christian beliefs.

STUDENT
STRIKE
• • • • • • •

*For unto you it is given in the
behalf of Christ, not only to
believe on Him, but also to
suffer for His sake.
Philippians 1:29*

Allahabad University is a large, residential university. I attended it with nearly five thousand select students from all over India. Out of the five thousand
students there were only twenty-two who professed
to be Christians. And of these twenty-two, probably
only three of us were born-again believers in Christ.

Soon after arriving at the university I told the
other Christian students that we ought to be witnessing for our faith among the Hindus and Muslims. But
they told me to keep my mouth shut.

"You are here to study. You have no reason to
disturb the peace. You will get some very violent
reactions," they warned. Nevertheless, I had a great

desire to share my life-changing faith in Christ with fellow students.

During the spring of 1953 the communist faction of the student union organized an all-school strike. The purpose of the strike was to make the annual examinations a little easier. Allahabad had been known for the tough examinations they gave at the end of each year. During the year there was no pressure. No required assignments, not even a quiz or a test. But, as the Indian educational system dictated, at the end of the year the students had to take a final examination that would cover all the material studied over the entire year. If a student did not pass this examination, the entire year of classes would have to be repeated. So the students, tired of cramming at the last minute for that final examination, wanted to make the exam a little easier.

I did not approve of the idea of that strike. So I decided I would not join with the other students. News had gone out to the leaders of the student union that I was not going to participate.

On the morning the strike was to begin, I had my breakfast and came back to my room to study. Soon I heard a knock. I opened the door to find two strong young men from the student union. In threatening tones the bigger one said, "We understand that you are not going to join the strike."

I replied simply, "That's right."

They wanted to argue with me, but as far as I was concerned, there wasn't much to argue about. I held firm to my convictions, and obviously they weren't going to call off the protest on account of one small tribal student. As they left, I thought the matter was finished.

Fifteen minutes later, the two ruffians returned with three other big men. They threatened, "Join the strike, or else!" Their English was not very good, but they pronounced the "or else!" rather forcefully. They glared at me, then left. I knew something was going to happen. But I wasn't afraid. Even though I am small, and have never been known to possess great physical power, I do have a lot of willpower. I can stand, and I can die, for what I believe.

After several minutes I heard a lot of commotion outside. My door was closed but not locked. I had not bothered to lock or even latch it. I listened to the angry voices outside my door, and soon realized that they were talking about me. Before I had a chance to lock the door, a brick struck the door and flung it open. I stood behind a wall to the right of the door so the bricks would not hit me. Before I knew it, there were lots of bricks in the room.

I waited for five or six minutes, anticipating another attack. When I was sure they were all gone, I peered around the door. They had all left. I gather the bricks, piled them outside my room, swept the floor, and knelt down to pray. I got up from my knees a little after nine o'clock, the time I usually leave for school. I gathered my books and solemnly made my way toward the university.

Allahabad University is surrounded by brick walls with four main gates, one at each point on the compass. My dormitory was west of the university, so I usually entered through the western gate. As I approached the gate, I could hear the chanting mob of striking students. There must have been at least five hundred of them blocking that entrance to the university. They were stopping all the professors' and instructors' cars from entering the university compound.

Wanting to avoid a confrontation with the mob, I slipped through a smaller, pedestrian gate that was located one hundred yards from the main gate. I was not even a hundred feet into the school compound when suddenly two men came running up behind me and grabbed me by both arms. With a very firm grip, they escorted me back to the gate and threw me out onto the ground, scattering my books and papers. As I was trying to retrieve my books, a tall and muscular Punjabi strode over and stared down at me. He unfolded his big arms and poked his finger into my forehead, saying, "Don't you know we communist students who organized this strike are willing to write our convictions with our blood? You shouldn't defy us!"

I pretended I didn't hear him. Again he poked me hard on the forehead and repeated his threat. Still I ignored him. The third time he repeated his threat, he poked me so hard I almost lost my balance. I looked up at him and said, "Look, if you communists are willing to write your convictions with your blood, I am willing to do even more. I am willing to spill every bit of blood I have in me for the cause I believe in. I am a follower of Jesus Christ, the man of peace. I know that He wouldn't join this strike if He were living on earth today." I kept looking right into that man's eyes. Finally he blinked and turned his head. I said, "Will you give me back my books?" The fellow who had my books handed them to me. I turned around and walked back through the gate into the university compound. This time nobody followed me.

I walked into the classroom and sat down. I was all alone. No one came in, not even the professor. I stayed there in the classroom until after noon, reading my New Testament and praying. I was struck with the words of the Apostle Paul: "For unto you it is given in the behalf of Christ, not only to believe, but to suffer for His sake." (Phil 1:25) Our willingness to suffer for Him takes away fear and instills the blessed joy.

When I went back to the dormitory, my Christian friends flocked around me in the corridor. They wondered how I could possibly stand against such an onslaught of communists. I told them that we have to stand for what we believe or we will always be consumed by those who will deprive us of our rights, our positions and our possessions.

From that time on, no one ever mistreated me at Allahabad University. Not one student wasn't aware of the fact that there was one small tribal student from northeast India who was a Christian and not ashamed of his faith. The professors treated me with new respect. Everywhere I went, they said, "He's a Christian."

The most beautiful thing happened a week later. The big Punjabi who had poked me came to my room and said, "I want to know where you get that courage."

"It's from the God of the Bible," I told him. I picked up my Bible and let it fall open. "You see, I am a tribal man and my forefathers were headhunters, but years ago God changed my father from being a headhunter to being a heart-hunter. This change came about when he read the story of Jesus Christ in a Bible.

"I have also experienced this change of heart that came from knowing the Lord Jesus. Let me read you one of my favorite verses, John 3:16: 'For God so loved the world, that He gave His only begotten Son, that whosoever believeth in Him should not perish, but have everlasting life.'"

The Punjabi seemed sincere and open as he asked many questions. It was plain he was seeking the truth. After much discussion we knelt down and prayed that he too might know Jesus Christ, the Son of the living God, as his personal Savior.

I was filled with joy that God had given me the opportunity to share my faith with this ringleader of the strikers.

GLASGOW,
GLASGOW

• • • • • • •

*In all thy ways acknowledge Him,
and He shall direct thy paths.*
Proverbs 3:6

I had just finished my final year at the University of
Allahabad when I was granted an audience with the
prime minister of India, Pandit Jawaharlal Nehru. I
told Prime Minister Nehru about the plight of the
Hmar people. Within a 4,000-square-mile area, there
was no post office. My father had to walk more than
eighty miles on foot in order to post a letter. I asked
the prime minister to come to our rescue, to provide
us with communication facilities. He suggested that
I get in contact with the civil service of the government and recommended that I meet with Dr. Verrier
Elwin, adviser to the government of India on tribal
affairs.

Nehru asked me where he could get in touch
with me once I returned to the hills of Manipur. I told
him where I could be found in the capital city of

Imphal.

Two days after I arrived in Imphal, a government messenger came with a summons for me to go to the Circuit House, a sort of hotel where high government officials stay when traveling on business. I went to the Circuit House with two of my friends. When we arrived, we were greeted by the postmaster general for northeastern India, who had come from Shillong. He said that he had received a message from the prime minister about the lack of post offices in our district. The postmaster had decided to open four post offices in our area and, since he was not familiar with the Manipur hills, he wanted me to suggest four suitable locations. Each post office was to have one delivery a week. I was overjoyed at this progress for our people. Then, to my further surprise, he asked me to recommend four postmasters, one in each of the towns.

My friends looked at me in disbelief. When I reached my home village, Phulpui, I found the news of my successes had preceded me. That was the closest I'd ever come to being a celebrity! My parents beamed.

"We must praise the Lord for the opportunities He has sent you," my father said.

A delegation of the tribal leaders, many much older than my twenty-seven years, asked me to start and head up a political movement. They said, "You are already known to the prime minister and leaders of this land. But our tribe is not known by the government. We have no schools and no roads. Our system of slash-and-burn cultivation is destroying the land. There are so many things we need, so many improvements we must have. We need a voice."

But my father wasn't so anxious for me to become a politician. He was unhappy because the whole Bible had not yet been translated into the Hmar language – and that had been the reason for my education. Bible translation was the purpose my father had dedicated me to fulfill; it was the reason my parents had sacrificed so much to support me. So I was reluctant myself to become too involved in politics.

Nevertheless, I wanted to serve my people. But which was better, politics or Bible translation?

My mother prayed. Then she said, "God knows everything. If it is wrong for you to start a political movement, God will not let you go so far as not to find your way back. He will turn it around." With this assurance I left for the convention the leaders had called.

It was the first political convention ever for the Hmar tribe. Hundreds of delegates from all over our land came together in Parbung, one of the larger Hmar villages. The place was full of excitement. I soon discovered that my people can be very rowdy.

On the first night of the convention, one of the elders stood up and spoke to the people in the most flowery language I had ever heard. I had never known any of our people to have that kind of ability. He told the people what a great fellow I was, so great that even the prime minister of India listened to me. He said, "We have just one man and one man only. One man in all of northeastern India who has the ear of the prime minister. Rochunga Pudaite."

The elders ushered me to the podium. The crowd cheered and called for a speech. I didn't quite know what to say. I told them that I had felt so inadequate when I met the prime minister that I was shivering. I said that I wasn't one of those big shots, but that I spoke only because of the needs of our people. The crowd was enthusiastic and gave me a standing ovation.

On the second day of the convention we discussed all that the party was going to do in the future. We prepared a beautiful outline of our program for the next ten years. I presented this program to the convention that night. They shouted and cheered. It was very exciting for a recent college graduate to see that kind of reaction, to feel that kind of power. The next day the first election was held for the position of president of the Hmar National Congress. Needless to say, I was elected unanimously.

That evening I was to give an acceptance speech and outline my immediate goals for the Hmar tribe. In order to prepare for it I isolated myself for three hours, putting my thoughts together. The head councilman of the village made a special dinner for me in his home. He killed the "fatted calf," invited all the leaders and prepared an impressive feast.

Just as we sat down to eat, someone came rushing into the house, carrying a message for me. I opened the bundle and found four letters inside. I opened the one from my father first. It said that a messenger had come carrying the letters all the way

from Lakhipur. He had thought they must be important, and sent them on to me immediately.

I opened the second letter. It was from the prime
minister's daughter, Mrs. Indira Gandhi. In a handwritten letter, she congratulated us and wished us
every success. The third one was from Governor
Jairam Das Doulatram. It carried the big seal of the
governor of Assam. He, too, wished us well. The
fourth was a cable from a missionary leader in
Canada. It read:

MY FRIENDS AND I WILL PAY FOR INTEN-
SIVE BIBLE TRAINING IN LONDON OR GLAS-
GOW, SCOTLAND. CABLE DECISION.

I knew my father had seen that one. It had been
opened.

I was so troubled that I couldn't eat the lavish
meal in front of me. I tried hard to hide my emotions.
The men kept coming over to me, asking, "Why
aren't you eating? Can we bring you something else?
Are you well? Are you concerned about your speech
tonight?" Then they would reassure me, "There is
nothing to worry about. Everyone is for you.
Whatever you say, they are going to stand and
cheer."

Finally the dinner was over. I put my speech in
my jacket pocket and walked over to the convention
hall. I climbed onto the platform and the chairman
introduced me. I began, "Tonight, I am going to ask
for your indulgence. I am not going to give an
acceptance speech. I will leave that for tomorrow.

Tonight I will preach." The crowd hadn't expected a sermon, but I preached anyway. God was very real to me that evening while I was preaching. I read from the Lushai Bible and expounded on it for them. My message was very simple that night, but it was perhaps one of the most significant messages I have ever delivered.

Five of us had been staying in the home of Rev. Ruma, the pastor of the local church. The moon shone brightly as we walked back to his home. My friends were congratulating each other on how much we had accomplished in one day. I was silent.

When we arrived at the pastor's home, the others were tired and went to bed right away. I went to bed also, but could not sleep. There was struggle inside me that would not stop. I got up and walked around outside the house in the moonlight. The village was quiet. The silence was deafening. I returned to the house and lay down on the bed, but still sleep would not come.

Early the next morning, while it was still dark, I left the house. By the light of the moon, I made my way toward a road I had traveled many times when I was a boy. It was one or two miles from the village. When I had walked about a mile or so, I came to a deserted bamboo shed. The roof had collapsed and only one section of the floor remained. I went inside and sat down. I prayed, "Lord, what are you trying to say to me? Tell me what to do. If I reject the presidency, my people may lose hope, but if I remain here, I may never finish the Bible translation." I didn't hear any answer from Him.

The sun was just rising on the eastern horizon over the mountains. I fell flat on my face and said, "Lord, whatever you want to say to me, say it. I'll not say no to you." There was no audible voice, but deep down in my heart there was a still, small voice that said, *Glasgow, Glasgow.* As the "voice" continued, I felt fully assured this was a direct answer to my prayer.

I walked back toward my quarters, wondering. Who will lead my people? If only there had been someone well qualified to take my place, the decision would not have been so difficult. I knew the Lord was concerned for my people. He wanted what would be best for them in the long run, not just temporarily. Still, I didn't want them to feel I was turning my back on them.

My friends were still sleeping as I entered Rev. Ruma's home. I washed my face, drank a cup of tea, and began preparing a new speech to deliver that evening. It was very difficult, for I was turning my back on an opportunity for great power and fame, yet I felt compelled to follow God's leadership.

That was a long day. The hours seemed to drag on and on. It was hard to be enthusiastic about making plans for the future when I knew I would have no part in implementing them.

Time for the evening meeting finally came and I sat on the platform, waiting to make my announcement. Then some of the tribal leaders came to the front carrying a *puondum* cloth. My heart seemed to swell within me, making it difficult to breathe, for the *puondum* cloth was traditionally bestowed on tribesmen who had brought great honor to the tribe by their accomplishments. To merit this cloth was a fantasy of every Hmar.

I felt very humble as the leaders draped the red cloth with its black and white striped design upon my shoulders. "Now that you have finished your B.A. and distinguished yourself educationally, we bestow this cloth," the spokesman said. "You have brought honor to all Hmars, and we have confidence you will lead our tribe to greatness."

My heart was pounding furiously as they brought the feathered headdress that in times past had been given to great Hmar chiefs. As the long *vakul* feathers of the "king bird" were placed on my head, I prayed, *Oh, Lord, how can I turn my back on this mandate from my people? Are you sure you want me to leave?* Again the words *Glasgow, Glasgow* rang in my ears.

I cleared my throat before beginning to speak. Looking over the vast sea of eager faces, I sensed the feeling of anticipation that filled the hall. With trembling voice, I read the cable I had received and then said, "I am accepting this invitation from Watkin Roberts to study in Glasgow. Therefore, I humbly submit my resignation."

There was complete silence. The crowd that had been cheering me only moments before was stunned. I saw expressions of displeasure, of betrayal, of disillusionment. Seeing their reactions, I couldn't help but shed tears. "I do not know why I am doing this," I explained, "but God has spoken to me very clearly. I must go to Scotland."

The disapproval of my people was quite evident as I left the meeting and returned to the pastor's home. Quickly, I packed my belongings and left the house. I followed the forest trail I had walked with a hundred or more supporters earlier in the week. Now no friend stood with me, yet I was not alone. I knew that God was with me.

MONEY
IN THE BAG

• • • • • • •

There hath no temptation taken you
but such as is common to man:
but God is faithful, who will not suffer you
to be tempted above that ye are able;
but will with the temptation
also make a way to escape,
that ye may be able to bear it.
1 Corinthians 10:13

During the first week of August 1954, I went to Imphal to apply for my passport so that I could be in Scotland by the end of the month to begin my studies. When I arrived, I registered at the Guest House, a small lodge inside the city, where I had stayed two months earlier. After unpacking my suitcase, I went immediately to the passport office. The office had just closed, and the guard informed me that they would be open at ten the next morning.

"The passport officer, Mr. Thangkhopao Kipgen,

will be here then," he said.

I knew that name. I had been told that Mr. Kipgen was not a friend of my tribe, even though he was from a neighboring tribe. He had wanted the Hmars and other hill tribes to be registered with his tribe, the Kukis, in the national census. Mr. Kipgen had thought that he, being a leader among the Kukis, would have more power in the new democratic form of government if our tribes were counted together. The Hmar people had refused, and had been left out of the census altogether. Mr. Kipgen was not happy with us. Because his tribe was so close to ours, perhaps he was jealous of any progress we made.

I returned to the little hotel and had a good rest. Early the next morning I got up and prepared for my meeting with Mr. Kipgen. In the Guest House there was only one common restroom for the eight or nine lodgers. As I was cleaning up for my appointment, I saw a bag filled with crumpled newspapers beside the toilet. Absentmindedly, I reached in the bag and pulled out the papers to see what the news was. To my surprise, underneath the newspaper was a stack of one-hundred-rupee notes. I reached deeper into the bag and found that the bag was full of them. I looked at the bundle I had in my hand. It was real money. I quickly took the bag to my room and put it in my big suitcase. I knelt down beside my bed and prayed.

I wanted to keep the bundle; it contained more money than I had ever seen. I said, "Lord, what do you want me to do with this money? Shall I just keep it and not tell anyone?" It looked like a half million rupees ($125,000) or even more. I really could have used that money for God's work. I looked at the bundle again. Looking at my watch, I realized that it was already nine forty-five. I would have to take a rickshaw if I were to make my ten o'clock appointment.

As I was going downstairs, a man who had just gotten off a rickshaw came up the stairs, looking very distraught. He mumbled, "I'm dead! I'm dead! I'm finished! My life is finished!"

"Can I do something for you?" I asked him.

He did not respond. I watched as he stumbled into his room, right across the hall from mine. I turned and called the rickshaw he had just been riding. When I met the passport officer, Mr. Kipgen, he said, "Here is an application form. Fill it out. You will need two people to guarantee you. Both of them must have at least ten thousand rupees in the bank or they must be civil servants – gazetted officers – to qualify as guarantors."

I didn't know anyone who would fit that description, so I asked him, "Could you be one?"

"No!" he replied. "I cannot be because I am the grantor of the passport, but here are two names." He gave me the names of two civil servants that he knew.

I said, "I don't know them. What will I say? Can I tell them that you sent me? Could you please scribble a note that you are sending me to them?"

Mr. Kipgen obliged, and wrote a note that he was ". . . sending the bearer of this letter. Please do the needful for him." I thanked him properly. I was absolutely amazed how polite and gracious T.

Kipgen was.

My mind was on the money I had left behind in the Guest House as I took a rickshaw back to the hotel. When I entered I could hear the man across the hall groaning and weeping. I couldn't bear it. I knocked at his door and said, "Is there anything I can do for you?"

"Nothing! Nothing!" came the reply. "I'm dead! Don't trouble me! I'm finished." He slammed the door in my face.

I went into my room, opened the suitcase, and looked at the money. I went back across the hall to the man's room and knocked at his door. He answered, but seeing I was the same man, he didn't even open it wide enough for me to talk to him. He slammed it again. I went back to my room, looked at the money again, and waited for nearly an hour. Then I knocked at his door again. This time I didn't wait for an invitation. I pushed the door open and walked right in. I commanded, "Come to my room."

"No, I'll not leave this room," came his reply.

I literally pushed him out of the door and into my room. Then slowly, I pushed him near the suitcase and opened it. The man just about hit the ceiling.

"That's my money!" he cried. "That's my money! How did you get it?"

He told me that his father had sent him to transact a big business deal in Imphal. He was to make the payment in cash. The man was from a wealthy Marwari family in Calcutta.

The first thing he did was touch my forehead, saying, "Ram, Ram." Ram is a Hindu god. He touched my forehead again, fell down at my feet and kissed my toes. He was flat on his face, crying out, "Ram, Ram."

When he got up from the floor, he put his hand in the money bag and brought out a bundle. He said, "Take it! You saved my life."

"No," I protested. "I can't take it. It's your money."

"I was in such a hurry. I don't know what was on my mind," he explained. "I went to the restroom and left in such a hurry. I hopped into a rickshaw that was waiting for me. By the time I realized the money bag was not with me, I was far away from the hotel. I came back but it was gone." Finally he asked, "What is your religion? Your God can be trusted. No other God would do this. He must be very good." I proceeded to tell him about my God.

I remembered the piece of paper in my hand with the two names on it. I visited them and said that Mr. Kipgen had sent me with the application form for them to sign. They both signed it. When I went back to Mr. Kipgen at four in the afternoon, he couldn't believe it. He exclaimed, "It's remarkable! It's surprising they signed for you. Come back a week from tomorrow," he continued, "and I'll have your passport ready for you." No one that I know has ever obtained a passport in India in less than one month. I got it the next week.

I felt doubly blessed that day. Not only had I gotten the signatures I needed, but also I had been given the strength to return the bag of money. The temptation to keep it had been great, but God had provided a way of escape.

COALS
OF FIRE

• • • • • • •

If thine enemy hunger, feed him;
if he thirst, give him drink:
for in so doing, thou shalt heap
coals of fire on his head.
Romans 12:20

I had been in Scotland for eight months and was very excited about the work I was doing. The translation of the New Testament into the Hmar language was going well, and my classes in Greek and Hebrew, though difficult, were shedding new light on many verses of Scripture.

The British and Foreign Bible Society had their headquarters in London. Dr. William Bradnock was the translation secretary. His wife was a medical doctor, and they had been missionaries in the Indian state of Punjab. Dr. Bradnock was very interested in my work. I always enjoyed being with him.

During the spring vacation in 1955, Dr.

Bradnock invited me to spend a weekend in his country home outside London. I didn't want to miss the opportunity to get away and spend time with the Bradnocks, so I took an overnight bus from Glasgow to London, and a taxi to Victoria Station, where I would board a train for the Bradnocks' home in Kent.

It was about eight in the morning when I climbed aboard the train and walked into a compartment. It was empty except for one man facing me on the right side of the seat. He was reading a newspaper. Having traveled all night on the bus, I thought I was fortunate to have a chance to stretch out for the hour-long train ride. I sat down and opened my Bible. I had not yet finished my reading when a sophisticated-looking English lady, wearing a heavy fur coat, entered our compartment. A porter followed her with two heavy suitcases and placed them on the luggage rack above the seat. The train whistled and we began to move.

I was still reading my devotion when the lady looked at me and asked, "Where do you come from?"

"From India," I replied. I didn't know I had said anything wrong until the lady launched into a verbal assault on me.

"You people come from a poor country," she began. For the next fifteen minutes my ears were pierced with some of the hardest English language I had ever heard. The flow of abusive language never relented as she made sure I knew all the benefits I was enjoying in her country. She ended her flurry by saying, ". . . and my husband has to pay the tax!"

I had no idea how much I had been taking England for granted, with all the education, medical and transportation facilities. There were more facilities in England than I ever imagined, and I realized that I was enjoying them without even knowing it.

I didn't know exactly how to respond. I thought for a moment and politely asked, "Madam, if I had not come here, would your husband be exempt from paying tax?" It seemed like an appropriate question to ask.

The man reading the newspaper brought it closer and closer to his face. The lady unleashed another verbal assault that slashed me for thirty minutes. It was incredible! I tried repeatedly to interrupt. "Madam, I'm sorry." But there was no way I could stop her. So I just kept saying, "I'm sorry! I'm sorry!"

Finally we arrived in Croydon, the stop before Kent. The British lady got up and walked out, looking for a porter to carry her luggage. Somehow, she was unable to find one. I knew that the train would soon be leaving, so I took down the two heavy suitcases and carried them out. The lady was still looking for a porter when she saw me carrying the suitcases over to the lounge area. She came over to where I stood. I looked up at her and said, "My dear lady, I'm truly grateful for the privilege of being with you. It's so easy to take things for granted, things that I have enjoyed in England. Others have had to suffer to give them to us. I'm grateful to God and I'm grateful to you. God bless you."

I left the luggage and walked back to the train. As I was climbing onto the train, I noticed that the lady had followed me. She stopped me and said, "I have never met a man like you." The tone of her voice was completely changed. Kindly, she added, "You are the most peculiar man I have ever met."

"Thank you so much," I replied. "God bless you." The train whistled and I stood at the door watching the lady. She pulled out her handkerchief and waved it at me.

"God bless you, too," she called. I was amazed.

People say there are coincidences. But I don't believe that. For when the lady came into the room I was reading Romans 12. The last part of the chapter, beginning with verse 17, says, "Recompense to no man evil for evil. Provide things honest in the sight of all men. If it be possible, as much as lieth in you, live peaceably with all men. Dearly beloved, avenge not yourselves, but rather give place unto wrath: for it is written, Vengeance is mine; I will repay, saith the Lord. Therefore if thine enemy hunger, feed him; if he thirst, give him drink; for in so doing thou shalt heap coals of fire on his head. Be not overcome of evil, but overcome evil with good."

I thank God for giving me the grace not to answer but rather listen to her. I am sure her burden, whatever it was, was lightened. For the Bible says, *A soft answer turns away wrath* and I know how true God's Word is. (Proverbs 15:1)

NEW SHOES

• • • • • • •

Thy shoes shall be iron and brass;
and as thy days,
so shall thy strength be.
Deuteronomy 33:25

When the first snow fell over Scotland, I was excited! It was the first time I had ever seen snow, except for on the distant peaks of the Himalayas. I wanted to walk all over the snow, and I did. I soon discovered that Indian shoes were not made for snow. My feet became very wet and cold. I wanted to dry them, but they were the only pair of shoes I had. I had to wear them even though they were wet.

A few days later, the soles of the shoes fell off. I tied them back on so that I could at least go down to the store and buy a new pair. I went to many shoe stores in Glosgow, but everywhere I went the salesmen would say, "We don't make size five-and-a-half anymore in men's shoes."

I went from store to store, and the answer was the same. "We don't make size five." I came back to my room discouraged. I had bought canvas shoes while I was in India – "sneakers," as they are called in America. So I began wearing them. I had to wear my sneakers even to church. They did very little to protect my feet against the cold climate. I had to have a new pair of shoes.

I went to all the stores again. They advised me to go to the boys' shoe department, but boys' shoes do not fit men's feet. They are shaped differently. I was getting very frustrated.

Finally, I couldn't keep my discouragement to myself anymore. I went to the principal of the school, Dr. McBeth, and explained my dilemma. Dr. McBeth was a man of compassion and prayer. He told us many times how God answered his prayers when he was a missionary in Africa. I asked him to pray for me.

Dr. McBeth agreed, "Sure. Let's pray." So we prayed. Then he volunteered, "Let me take you to a store. I know exactly where they will have the kind of shoes you need." He proceeded to take me to a store where I had already been. I told Dr. McBeth that I had already tried that store. He said, "Well, let me take you to another one."

When we went to the next store, they recognized me. "He's been here," they told Dr. McBeth. So we went to another store. It was the same story.

Then Andrew McBeth looked at me and said, "How about boys' shoes?" Well, I didn't smile.

"Let's go home," I told him. I had tried the boys' shoes, and they didn't fit. I wasn't about to try them again. So we went home. For another week I walked around Scotland in my sneakers.

One day I said to myself, "I'm going to try again." I prayed all morning. Finally, I took courage and left the dormitory. I went down to Queen's Street to the same big shoe store near Burton's Men's Shop. It was one of the biggest shoe stores. I walked right in.

A new salesman greeted me. I told him, "I would like to buy a pair of shoes."

"All right. What size?" he asked. I told him my size and he said, "Let me go and see." He came back and said, "We don't carry that size anymore." Then the other salesman I had spoken to before came up.

He recognized me. "You have been here twice before. We don't have shoes in your size. I wish we had some to sell you."

"But I think you ought to have them," I argued.

"You know we would love to sell you a pair of shoes, but we don't have your size," he countered.

I looked at him firmly and said, "You ought to have them."

The manager of the store came out and asked his salesmen, "What is he talking about?"

I turned to him and said, "Sir, I think you have my shoes here. I came to get them."

The man looked at me and looked at my feet. "What size shoes do you wear?" he asked.

"Size five," I replied. "But if you don't have five, maybe I can stretch to a five and a half."

He said, "Will you wait just a moment?" He turned to the salesman and said, "You remember there was a wealthy Spanish fellow who had small feet? We had handmade shoes for him, and I don't think he picked up his last pair. They have been here for a long time. Let me go back and see what happened to them." The manager went to the back room and came back with a pair of shoes.

He opened the box and I looked at them. They were beautiful. I didn't want to ask what size they were. I said, "May I try them on?" I put them on and they fit just as though they were made for my feet. I said, "What's the price?"

"About one hundred pounds!" was the reply. In those days, a pound was worth $2.71.

I just looked at my feet and said, "Well, they just fit." The manager kept looking at me and I didn't say anything more.

"Sonny, how much money do you have?" he asked. I pulled out all the money I had in my pocket. It was twelve pounds. He looked at me for a long time, then he said, "Take them home with you."

I didn't even put them back in the box. I left the store wearing my beautiful new shoes. I couldn't wait to walk up the steps of 64 Bothwell Street, where Dr. McBeth lived. I rushed up and knocked at the door. Dr. McBeth answered. I stood silently; I wasn't going to say anything. He was puzzled. Suddenly he looked down and saw the beautiful pair of shoes. He went down on his knees.

"Let's thank God," he said. Only after he prayed did he ask how I got my shoes.

I went back to my room and opened the Bible to Deuteronomy. "Thy shoes shall be made of iron and brass; and as thy days, so shall thy strength be," read verse 25 of chapter 33. God had given me the best leather shoes, strengthened by iron and brass. These shoes would neither slide nor spoil in the snow. God knew my need, and He provided.

CALIFORNIA
TRIP

• • • • • • •

Take no thought, saying, what shall we eat?
Or, what shall we drink?
Or, wherewithal shall we be clothed? . . .
Your heavenly Father knoweth that ye
have need of all these things.
Matthew 6:31-32

I came to the United States in September 1955. Soon after I arrived, I received a letter from a retired missionary friend, Paul Rostad. Paul and his wife Ella had been missionaries in India for many years. When Ella died of cancer while in India, Paul had become very lost and lonely. I had been the last one to see him off from Calcutta on his way back to America.

Paul's letter invited me to go and spend Christmas with him in California. He was living in Santa Barbara at the time.

I replied immediately. I said I would be glad to travel to his home during the Christmas vacation.

Paul sent me enough money to get to California by bus. When I inquired at the Greyhound station how long the trip would take, I decided that I would add a little money of my own and go by train.

I wrote a letter to Dr. Bob Pierce, who had brought me to the United States. He and his family were also living in California and I thought I'd try to see him. Dr. Bob was one of the busiest men among mission leaders. He traveled so much that it was difficult to make plans to see him in the U.S. It was easier for me to see him when he visited Asia. In my letter, I mentioned that I would be arriving on the train at four-thirty in the morning in Los Angeles, and that from there I was going on to Santa Barbara by bus.

I was amazed at how fast the American trains ran. I was also surprised at how few stops we made between Chicago and Los Angeles. I arrived in L.A. promptly at four-thirty in the morning. It was still dark. I had no idea where the bus station would be, but I knew I could find my way. I picked up my suitcase, and got off the train. Who was there waiting for me but Dr. Bob Pierce! It must have taken him an hour to drive down from his home, but there he was!

Dr. Bob came over and hugged me. "Buddy, how good it is for me to welcome you to Los Angeles." I'll never forget that. Then he said, "You are not going on to Santa Barbara right away, are you?"

"That was my plan," I replied.

He looked at me again and said, "Look, let's do this. There is a Plaza Hotel in Hollywood. I'll drive you there and check you in. Stay for a day or two here and then you can go on to Santa Barbara."

"Whatever you say, Dr. Bob," I replied.

He checked me into the Plaza Hotel. It was still early in the morning.

"Go get your luggage," he said. "Freshen up a bit and come back. We'll have breakfast together." I came down at six o'clock wearing my old spare suit from my suitcase. I found him at the telephone booth. He was already on the phone, talking to some of his friends on the east coast.

After we had breakfast he said, "Rochunga, I'm going to wait a little while so that I can take you to a men's clothing store. If you are going to visit your missionary friend, you better look a little more presentable. You can't go like that."

"I'm all right," I replied, self-consciously.

"No, I want to take care of you. Why don't you go up to your room and take a little nap. I will wake you at nine o'clock and we'll go to the men's store. I want to buy you a new suit." I obeyed him; I returned to my room and took a nap.

A while later he took me out to a men's store. As we walked in, he said to the manager, "I have a friend here from India. I would like you to outfit him with a new suit."

The man came over, looked at me, measured me, and said, "I don't think we have any men's suits that will fit him. But let me check anyway," he suggested. We looked all over the store; there wasn't a single suit in my size.

Dr. Bob took me to a second men's store in Hollywood but they didn't have anything either.

"We don't have anything smaller than size 40,"

we were told. I needed size 38. Then Dr. Bob Pierce held my hand and looked up at the ceiling of the store and said, "Lord, you've got to help us. I want to give my friend a new suit, but we can't find one. Tell us where to go now." He really cried out to God. The manager and the salesgirls must have wondered what in the world this man was doing in the middle of their store. But Dr. Bob didn't seem to care.

After Dr. Bob prayed, the manager came back and said, "Just a minute. There was a fellow from Mexico who used to buy clothes from us. He was a man with fine taste, and he was also just the size of your friend. We used to tailor-make suits for him. I think we still have a suit he never picked up. If you'll wait, I'll get it for you." He disappeared into the back room again and emerged with two beautiful custom-tailored suits, one blue and one gray. I tried one on and it fit perfectly. It seemed as if it were made especially for me. Dr. Bob looked at me and lightly touched here and there. "Buddy, it fits you, doesn't it?"

I was overwhelmed. "I don't think I have ever had a suit that fits as well as this one," I replied.

"What's the price?" Dr. Bob asked the manager.

"$150 each," came the reply.

That was a lot of money in those days. That's still a lot of money. I said, "Dr. Bob, that's too much."

The man looked at me, then at Dr. Bob, and said, "Let me give you both suits for the price of one. How about that?"

Still I refused. "No. I have never owned two new suits in my entire life and I already have one here on my body. That is too much." But Dr. Bob Pierce insisted that I have the two beautiful new suits that fit me so well. All they had to do was hem the trousers.

"After such a long trip, you should go back and rest," Dr. Bob said. "This afternoon we'll pick up your suits, and then you can come to my home and meet my wife, Lorraine, and my children." At four that afternoon he picked me up and we went for the suits. We drove to his home and with his family put up the Christmas tree. It was the first time in my life I had ever helped decorate a Christmas tree.

"Now, about tomorrow," Dr. Bob said. "What do you want to see in Los Angeles?"

I replied, "Nothing, really. So long as I'm with you people, that's all I want. I don't even know what there is to see."

Dr. Bob knew that India produced more films even than Hollywood. "I think you would enjoy a tour of a movie studio," he said. The next morning, he had a friend drive me to the Paramount Studios where they were filming some kind of a love scene. It didn't appeal to me at all, and I walked out and went back to my hotel.

That afternoon I went to see the Cinerama. That really was something else. I had never seen anything like it. It made me feel like I was a part of the whole thing. I enjoyed immensely the scene in the Swiss Alps.

Dr. Bob and Lorraine took me out to dinner that evening. They dropped me at the hotel and the next day I took a bus on my way to Santa Barbara, feeling loved, rich and well-supplied.

As I rode along, I kept thinking how good God is. He provides all my needs so abundantly. What a blessing it was to have such a kind and generous friend as Dr. Bob. I wished I could repay him. I wished I could have enough money so I could give to others freely and be a blessing to my friends.

Paul Rostad was an elderly gentleman. He didn't own a car, so we took a taxi to his little apartment. When Paul was in India, he had a very big bungalow and four or five servants. I had been wondering what kind of place I would find him living in. I was surprised that he only had a tiny apartment: one bedroom, a dining area, a kitchen and a bathroom. He wanted to give me his bed and said he would sleep on the hide-a-bed. I had no idea what a hide-a-bed was, but I said, "If you have a hide-a-bed, I will sleep there."

In the evening, we pulled out the sofa, and there was the hide-a-bed I would sleep on. Again I wished I had money so that I could buy something nice for this dear friend's apartment, but I had so little.

That first evening, Mr. Rostad looked at me wistfully and asked, "Do you happen to know how to cook an Indian dinner?"

"I sure do," I replied. I could tell he was longing for an Indian meal. I felt so happy! Here was the opportunity to be a blessing to my friend. The next day while he was out, I went to the grocery store and bought all the necessary ingredients to cook an Indian meal. When he returned that evening, everything was ready. I had set the table as nicely as I could.

When he walked in, he smelled the aroma of Indian curry. I saw the smile on his face for the first time since I arrived at his home. He grinned. "It looks like you were doing something today."

"I did," I said, "and it's all ready."

He sat on his side of the table, reached over for my hand, and said, "I want to thank God." He prayed a beautiful prayer. As we enjoyed that humble meal I realized more than ever the truth of what our Lord Jesus taught, "It is more blessed to give than to receive," (Acts 20:35) and that we can give more than just money.

THE DIME
THAT LASTED
FOREVER

● ● ● ● ● ● ●

Wherefore lift up the hands which hang down,
and the feeble knees.
Hebrews 12:12

One beautiful spring morning in 1956 while a student at Wheaton College, I was delighted to receive a letter from Dr. Frank Phillips, executive assistant to Dr. Bob Pierce. He wrote that Dr. Bob was going to appear on a television show in Minneapolis, and that he wanted me to be on the program with him. Enclosed was a ticket to Minneapolis. I was very excited. I was to leave in three days, and was very anxious to see Dr. Bob again.

I had a little problem, though. I was broke. One of the policies I practiced while I was a student in America was that I never borrowed money. If I didn't have any money, I always worked for it. And if I still didn't have enough, I did without. That had been my principle.

It just so happened that the previous week had been my worst. I couldn't even get a baby-sitting job. Friday morning came and there wasn't a dollar in my pocket, just one dime. I was quite sure that when the mail came later that morning, there would be some money in it for me. After my nine o'clock class, I went to my mailbox and found it empty. I thought, hopefully, that the mail had not come in yet. I was sure that after the ten-thirty chapel there would be something there. According to the airline ticket, I had to be at Midway Airport for my flight at 1:30 P.M. But I had only one dime, not enough to get to the airport.

After chapel I eagerly went back to the mailbox. Nothing. I was a little shaken. I had a class at eleven, but I just could not proceed to the classroom. Knock-kneed, I went up the stairs of the Wheaton College Memorial Student Center. On the third floor there is a little prayer chapel. I entered the chapel and sat down in the second seat from the back. Kneeling on my knocking knees, I began to pray. I just couldn't miss the privilege of being with Bob Pierce in Minneapolis, yet I had no way of getting to the airport.

After praying for a while, I opened my Bible to read a portion for the day. My knees were still knocking and my heart was unstable; I began reading Hebrews 12. In verse 11 it says, "Now no chastening for the present seemeth to be joyous, but grievous: nevertheless afterward it yieldeth the peaceable fruit of righteousness unto them which are exercised thereby."

The next verse was the one that brought life back

to my heart: "Wherefore lift up the hands which hang down and the feeble knees." I don't know why, but the Bible always seems to come to me in my time of need, even with the exact words. My hands were hanging down because they were so weak. The verse spoke directly to me. I read on to the next two verses: "Wherefore lift up the hands which hang down and the feeble knees; And make straight paths for your feet, lest that which is lame be turned out of the way; but let it rather be healed."

I prayed, "Lord you have such a good sense of humor. You come through for me, I'll trust you and not be afraid. I'll go to Minneapolis, even if I have to walk to the airport." I came downstairs thanking God and went to Dr. Merrill C. Tenney's class.

Dr. Tenney looked at me as I walked in and said, "Well, you are a bit late, aren't you?" I said nothing and sat down in a chair near the back. By this time there was complete peace in my heart. Whether I went to Minneapolis or not didn't matter. God had dealt with me. That was the only important thing. I knew He loved me.

After class I dashed to the dining hall for a quick lunch. There was always a long line at noon. Just as I was going to pick up my tray, my friend Tom Howard and his girlfriend Lovelace came rushing in.

"Ro, do you mind if we go ahead of you?" Tom asked.

"Not at all," I replied. "Why are you in a hurry?"

Grabbing a tray and some silverware, Tom said, "I have to be at the airport by 1:34."

"Well, I have to be there at 1:30," I replied. "But go

ahead."

Looking at me he asked, "How are you going? Who is going with you?"

"I don't know yet."

"Would you like to ride with us? We can take you."

"You are going with your girlfriend. I don't want to intrude," I protested.

"Oh, come with us. That won't be a problem at all. We would love to have you," Tom was insistent.

Lovelace joined in, "That would be a joy. In fact, I have wanted to talk to you since you spoke in chapel."

"Well, if you insist, I'll go with you," I accepted.

We stopped at 103 N. President Street, where I was living, picked up my little suitcase, which I had packed that morning, and we were on our way. When we arrived at Midway Airport, I still had about ten minutes before the plane took off. As I reached the top of the ramp, I looked back and waved my hand to Tom and Lovelace.

Suddenly a man rushed up to me and called, "Ro, wait for me." It was George Wilson, Billy Graham's executive vice president and general manager. I had met George in London during the Billy Graham crusade. He approached me and shook my hand. "Dr. Bob Pierce spoke about you at the NAE convention in Buffalo. Everyone was so blessed and moved and challenged by your life. I said to myself, 'I wish I could meet Ro again.' I had no idea about your background when we met in London," he exclaimed. "If there are two seats together, would you mind sitting with me?" he asked.

"Not at all!"

As we walked into the plane, there just happened to be two seats vacant in one row. We had such an exciting conversation on the flight from Chicago to Minneapolis. We lost all track of time.

We were still talking while we waited for our luggage in the airport terminal. When our baggage arrived, George said, "I would like to finish this conversation. Do you mind if I drop you off at the hotel?"

"Wouldn't it be a little out of the way?" I politely asked. I had no idea how to get around Minneapolis, and I only had the one dime in my pocket anyway.

"It'll be no problem at all," he said. "The Curtis Hotel is right by the Billy Graham office. It will be a pleasure for me to drop you off." So we hopped into his car and drove to the hotel. I still had my dime.

When I arrived at the hotel, I picked up the telephone and called Dr. Bob. He came rushing down to the lobby and hugged me.

"Rochunga, what a pleasure, what a joy, what a blessing you are." He had no idea of the ordeal I had gone through that morning in trying to get to the airport, but, as always, he asked, "Do you have spending money?" I remained silent. Dr. Bob reached over and put fifty dollars in my coat pocket. "You might like to see some sights in Minneapolis, since you've not been here before," he said. "Let's go to my room and have prayer first. After we pray, have your meal and sign your name to the bill. That's all you need to do, just sign your name." And that's what I did.

That night, Dr. Bob spoke to a large Youth For Christ rally. He called on me to give my testimony. The next day, Sunday morning, we spoke at a large church.

The pastor, Rev. Peterson, had a television program called "Soul's Harbor." After the morning service, we went to the television station and did a half-hour television show. When we finished, George Wilson picked us up and took us to a beautiful country club for a late Sunday dinner.

I kept thinking of those beautiful Bible verses in Hebrews 12: "Wherefore lift up the hands which hang down, and the feeble knees; and make straight paths for your feet, lest that which is lame be turned out of the way; but let it rather be healed" (verses 12-13). How often we just need to go to God for our feeble knees to be made strong and for healing to come to our hanging hands.

I returned to Wheaton that evening. I still had my dime.

When I came back to Wheaton, I immortalized my little dime. "I'll never spend it until I go to heaven," I told my friends. "One thing I know for sure – God is God. My God is a living God. I can trust Him," I told them.

I wrote a little article for the college newspaper. I titled it "A Dime Lasts, Like the Widow's Cruse of Oil." On the day the article came out I received at least twenty telephone calls from fellow students who were struggling with their financial problems. What an encouragement it was to meet and pray with some of them.

Our God is able to deliver those who come to Him for deliverance.

MADE
IN HEAVEN
• • • • • • •

Being in the way, the Lord led me.
Genesis 24:27

In January 1958, four years after I left India, a copy
of *Inchuklai Nun*, a magazine for Hmar students,
came to me in Wheaton, Illinois. In the news I
noticed an article that said the first Hmar girl ever to
graduate from high school in Manipur was planning
to go to college at Shillong. I realized that this girl,
named Lalrimawi, had attended a month-long
English study I had conducted one summer five
years before. I had encouraged her at that time to
seek higher education. I was very pleased to learn
she had taken my advice. I wrote a letter to congrat-
ulate her, and enclosed a small gift.

A lovely thank-you letter came back, and we
began corresponding occasionally. In one of my letters I asked if she were having any problem as a
Protestant girl attending a Roman Catholic college
and if there was anything I could do for her. I also

sent her some books.

One day in the spring of 1958, I was feeling very low. I was frustrated over the tedious job of completing the translation of the Hmar New Testament. Furthermore, I had been away from home for four long years.

On that Saturday morning I awoke feeling dejected. I skipped breakfast and communed with myself while still in bed. Later I slipped down to my little office in the basement to wrestle in prayer. I picked up one devotional book after another, hoping for a verse of Scripture or a sentence from a sage that would renew my spirit. At lunchtime I heard the mailman ring the bell. I rose from my knees to get the mail. There was a letter from Lalrimawi, written in English. She acknowledged my letter, and then went on,

You asked me if I had problems. Yes, but I do not pray for an easy task and that all the barriers should be broken down for me. I only pray that God will give me the strength, in weakness His will to do, for He said, "My grace is sufficient for thee."

I was so deeply moved by her resolute faith that I felt ashamed. Why should I feel discouraged? Why should my heart be lonely when I had so much more than anyone else? A new sense of inspiration began to flow into the inner recesses of my soul. I went upstairs to my room, combed my hair, and walked jubilantly to lunch. Lalrimawi's words walked with me, and strangely warmed my heart.

Later I read Lalrimawi's letter again. I tried to frame her picture in my mind but could not imagine her luminous eyes smiling beneath her smooth braids of black hair. I searched through my files and found a picture of her and her friends, taken at Pherzawl in tribal costumes. She was about fifteen in the picture and now was almost twenty. What would she look like now?

Finally the translation of the Hmar New Testament was completed and the final manuscript mailed to the British and Foreign Bible Society for publication. I became more engrossed with my studies and speaking engagements for the new mission organization called Indo-Burma Pioneer Missions, which had been founded in Canada by Watkin Roberts.

A few weeks later a letter came from Dr. Bob Pierce.

Would you join our World Vision team conducting summer pastors' conferences in Japan, Taiwan, Singapore, Burma and India? All expenses will be paid, including a round-trip air ticket.

India! How wonderful! I could make a side trip to my home, and see my family, friends, and, of course, Lalrimawi. I was bubbling with enthusiasm.

Summer came roaring in. I left Wheaton for California and went on to Honolulu and Tokyo. In Tokyo, I met with some of the World Vision team and flew with them to Osaka, where the pastors' conference was being held.

After visiting Singapore, Thailand and Burma, we flew to Calcutta, India, where my father came for the pastors' conference. It was such a joy to see him again. After the conference my father and I returned to Manipur, where I was reunited with my mother, relatives and friends. After a couple of days I realized that my parents were anxious to have some time alone with me for a private talk, so I set aside some time just for them.

"My son, we are concerned about you," my mother explained frankly. "You are almost thirty-one years old and still unmarried. There are too many problems for a single man in the ministry. It is time for you to marry."

I was just about to tell them about Lalrimawi and the growing fondness I felt for her because of our exchange of letters, when Mother surprised me with a question: "Have you met a college girl named Lalrimawi? She is now studying in Shillong. She came here last year for the students' conference. We liked her very much."

"Oh, Mother!" I blurted with mock indignation. "Shillong is three or four hundred miles away. What would the church leaders think of my going so far to see a girl?" Deep in my heart I longed to see her, but at that moment the way seemed impossible. Actually, I had invited Lalrimawi to come to Manipur during her vacation in October. But I had received a letter from her thanking me for my kind invitation, but firmly stating that she did not feel it would be proper for her to come to visit me. I shared my thoughts with my parents, but tried not to sound serious, since Lalrimawi and I had not seen each other for five years. In prayer we committed the matter to God.

I had planned for a trip to Silchar, Aizawl, Lakhipur, Phulpui, Senvon and many other villages in the interior parts of the Manipur hills. The trip was to start by the middle of November. A visit to Shillong and the possibility of meeting Lalrimawi seemed remote.

I was getting ready for the long journey when a letter came inviting me to speak in Shillong for the Bible Translators' Conference to be held November 6-9. The Bible Society would pay for my travel and lodging.

It seemed like a miracle. I wouldn't need to change my touring program. It was too good to be true! "Thank you, Lord . . . ." I prayed.

I sent a message to the leader of the Hmar Students Association to arrange a meeting for all the Hmar students in Shillong at the elegant Morello Tea Room the evening of November 5th. I thought surely Lalrimawi would be there that night, and I would meet her in the crowd.

About thirty-five Hmar students and government employees attended the meeting, but not Lalrimawi. I wondered what in the world had happened to her. Later I took a taxi to St. Mary's College, but the gate was already closed. I stood there in the flickering shadow of a dim light, looking through the bars at the dormitory. So near, yet so far . . . .

I returned the next day and asked for her. The mother superior, an Irish Catholic nun, wanted to know if I was related to her. I made a long story, and finally the nun said, "OK, but only ten minutes."

Taking a seat in the austere parlor, I waited impatiently. Suddenly I caught sight of a beautiful young lady wearing a Hmar tribal cloth and white embroidered blouse. She walked toward me. I rose to my feet in recognition.

She smiled and my heart skipped a beat. She looked beautiful, innocent, unsophisticated and wholesome. I moved toward her and without any display of outward affection, I shook her hands in greeting. For a long while we simply looked into each other's eyes.

There was so much to talk about. The "ten minutes" stretched into an hour, but the supervising nun did not intervene. Our conversation was laced with gentle laughter and quiet talk.

For some inexplicable reason I knew she was *the girl* God had chosen for me. As we talked I felt that here was a girl I could fully trust. I had to be bold and trust her to understand, I decided, then told her firmly, "I came to see if you might be God's choice for me."

I noticed the surprise that flickered in her eyes, and the delicate coloring in her cheeks.

"I will pray," she whispered sweetly.

"Before leaving," I said, "do you mind if I call you Mawii (meaning 'beautiful one')? It is so appropriate." She blushed in approval.

That evening I saw her again, this time in the company of a guardian appointed by her brother. Again the time rushed by, and I had to say good-bye.

The next day was a busy day at the translators' conference, but I made time for personal business. In keeping with our tribal custom, I discussed a possible marriage with a distant cousin, Mr. Thangsei, a civil servant who happened to be in town from another state. I sent him with a letter addressed to Lalrimawi:

November 7, 1958

My dear Mawii:

Mr. Thangsei was here 'til late into the night and we were discussing something wonderful.
Sunday seems to be very far away, as though in another century. I wish a day could be skipped! . . . I would be the happiest man in this hemisphere if our loving Father would join the two of us to one.

Lovingly,
Rochunga

P.S. Could I hear from you?

Mawii sent back word through my "emissary" that she was definitely praying about the marriage proposal.

For our first date, I invited her to go canoeing on the beautiful Ward Lake in front of the hotel. Though it was winter, the weather was unusually warm and clear. I lazily paddled the boat across the smooth water as we talked and laughed.

Blind to the curious onlookers on shore, she read

to me from *Tlangchar Tuihnar (Mountain Spring)*, the devotional book I had written, released only a few weeks earlier. The words sounded so pleasant and captivating that I could hardly believe I had written them.

Finally, I could hold my heart no longer, and I implored, "Mawii, will you marry me?"

"I have been praying about it, Rochunga. You see, several years ago I heard you preach. I told the Lord that if He would have me marry someday, I prayed it would be a man like Rochunga. It was my hope to marry a man who loves God as you do, but I thought it would be someone *like* Rochunga, and not Rochunga himself. It is God's way of answering my prayers even beyond my hopes. Now I see how the Lord has worked His plan to bring us together, and I will be happy to be your wife if my parents approve."

According to our tribal custom, I sent my older brother, Ramlien, and my brother-in-law, Luoia, to ask Mawii's parents for permission for me to marry their daughter. Since Mawii's village, Khawlien, was about a two-day journey from Senvon where I was to preach on November 30th, we agreed that they should send me word at Senvon.

On Monday, before I left Shillong, I sent a telegram to my parents in Sielmat, and to Dr. Bob Pierce:

BEING IN THE WAY, THE LORD LED ME. LETTER FOLLOWS.

These were the same words Abraham's servant

spoke when he found Rebekah to be Isaac's wife.

As I left Shillong in the evening for a long journey to Haflong, Silchar, Aizawl, and then into the interior hill villages of Manipur, I felt for the first time the bittersweet ache of romantic loneliness. But my heart was full and satisfied. God has shown me *the* girl, and she has said yes.

Twenty-one days after I left Mawii, while I was preaching on a Sunday night to a large audience at Senvon, a flashlight Morse-code signal came across the hill from Khawlien. *We are successful.* When the service was over, I returned a message: *Well done. Waiting for you here.*

Nearly two months after our meeting in Shillong, Mawii and I were married. The service was held on New Year's Day, 1959, on the 150th anniversary of the William Carey Baptist Church in Calcutta. Rev. Walter Corlett, my pastor from student days in Calcutta, performed the ceremony.

We spent our first night together in Calcutta. The next day we took a train for Madras to attend the World Congress on Christian Youth, where I spoke. From Madras we traveled to Vellore, where I spoke for one week at the famous Christian Medical College and Hospital founded by Dr. Ida Scudder. Finally we traveled home to Sielmat, where I introduced Mawii to my family and friends.

My mother beamed when she met Mawii. When she heard how God brought us together, she brightly said, "This marriage is made in heaven."

It truly was, and is, because God gives the best to those who leave the choice to Him.

RED LODGE
• • • • • • •

Let your moderation be known
unto all men. The Lord is at hand.
Philippians 4:5

It was the summer of 1971. I told Mawii and our three children that we were going on a vacation. We were going to drive and see America. I called a number of pastors I knew and told them that we would cook an Indian dinner in their churches and have dinner together with their congregations.

We started out by going to Iowa. Then we moved on to Minnesota and North and South Dakota, then on to Washington State, Oregon and California. We would be a month and a half on the road.

At one point, we were going to take a break from the dinner meetings and drive to Yellowstone Park. Our car was a Pontiac Tempest, one I had been using for four years. I had wanted to buy a new car before we left, but Mawii had disagreed. She felt the car still looked good. We had put more than 90,000 miles on the car, so I felt a little uneasy. I didn't know very much about mechanics, and was very reluctant to drive so far from home with an old car. By the time we reached Montana, the car had almost 100,000 miles.

We drove down from Billings one morning and the car started to act up. I began to murmur, "You know, this car is not going to make it. I wish we had bought a new car." A little down the road, the car stopped completely. I was able to start it up again, but the engine did not sound right.

We drove slowly into a town called Red Lodge. It is here that the mountains begin. We saw a Texaco gas station with a sign that said *Mechanic on Duty*. The mechanic looked at the car and said, "If I were you, I wouldn't travel any farther with this car. You have a broken piston!" I asked how long it would take to repair the car. He said, "We'll have to order the part from Billings and install it. It will probably take two days."

We sat in the car and discussed our dilemma. I began to fume a little that Mawii should have listened to me. The children were silent. I didn't know what we were going to do. Across the street there was another gas station, with another *Mechanic on Duty* sign. I decided to go across the street and see what that mechanic had to say. Perhaps *he* would know what to do.

The mechanic listened carefully to the sound of the engine. I turned off the engine, then tried to start the car again. But the car failed to start. He brought another mechanic over, started the car and decided it was a broken piston. It should take a full day, if not two, to repair, he said. By this time we had waited two hours. I was quite mad. *If only Mawii had listened to me before we left!* I thought. I asked the mechanics, "What would be the best thing to do?"

They replied, "Well, if you are in a great hurry, you can go back to Billings, although we don't know if the car will take you that far. The Pontiac dealers there may have the spare part to repair it in one day."

After a long while inside the car, I turned to my family and said, "Well, let's try to make it to Billings."

Mawii said, "Let's pray first." I didn't feel like praying. I was very upset. We should have used common sense and bought a new car before we left. Then we wouldn't have had this problem. *There are times you don't have to pray,* I thought. *You just use common sense.* So I didn't want to join the prayer.

Mawii said to the children, "Close your eyes, I'm going to pray." She prayed a simple prayer asking God for forgiveness in upsetting me and she asked God for a miracle for the car. After the prayer was over I waited a while and turned toward Billings. We had been in Red Lodge for three hours, fuming and getting nowhere.

As we turned around from Red Lodge to return to Billings, I saw an automobile dealer with used cars. Somehow I felt that I should pull in. It was just before the lunch hour. I pulled into the used-car lot and called a mechanic to come over. The mechanic said, "We were just about ready to go to lunch, but let me listen to the engine." After listening to the car for a minute, he said, "You know, I don't think it's a broken piston. Do you live near a city?"

"Yes," I replied.

The mechanic said, "Sometimes, when you don't drive in the country a lot, carbon builds up in the engine and it makes a sound just like this." He continued, "It so happens, two weeks ago a fellow from Chicago had this same problem and I put some engine cleaner fluid in. A lot of smoke was emitted when he ran the engine at regular speed, but after that it started to run as smoothly as a new car. Why don't we try it?" he offered. "If it is a broken piston, it won't do any damage."

The mechanic poured in a quart of engine cleaner fluid. He told me, "Start driving at thirty miles per hour through town, but as soon as you get out of the city, go up as fast as you can – fifty or sixty miles per hour – and see what happens."

I pulled out of the driveway and drove steadily through the city. As I stepped up to fifty miles per hour, thick black smoke began to pour from our exhaust pipe. By the time I reached seventy mph, the cloud of smoke filled the rear view mirror. Then suddenly the smoke stopped. I gently brought the car to a stop. The engine was as quiet as can be.

I returned to Red Lodge and thanked the man. He said, "There are a few little touches before you go on your way. For example, we must change the oil. Why don't you have lunch and I'll take care of it. Then you can go on to Yellowstone Park."

So we went to the Red Lodge restaurant. Everyone was smiling except me. I had a little difficulty in smiling, even though I was happy. I regretted not joining in prayer before. My guilty conscience was pricking at me.

The menu in the restaurant had everything Mawii and I had wanted to try: venison, buffalo, moose, elk and trout. Mawii ordered the venison and I had buffalo. Paul, John and Mary just wanted hamburgers.

We had a magnificent time at Yellowstone Park. Our car kept running all the way to Seattle, Washington, down the coasts of Oregon and California, across the Southwest, and all the way back to Wheaton. I kept that car for another year, never having any major problems.

God answers prayer. As the father of the house, I should have said, "Let us pray." But I hadn't. I had fumed and gotten angry. I needed to be reminded that nothing is too insignificant to take to the Lord.

THE BLIND JEEP

• • • • • • •

Call unto Me, and I will answer thee,
and show thee great and mighty things,
which thou knowest not.
Jeremiah 33:3

In 1972 God gave me a vision about reaching the world with the gospel by mailing Bibles to every person on earth who is listed in the telephone books. Since that time I have devoted my life to this ministry, but my heart has never been far from my Hmar people back in the hills of Manipur.

In 1981 and 1982 stories of great hunger in Manipur began reaching me. These accounts touched my heart and I began praying that God would provide food for my people.

There had been a two-year drought. People in the twenty-seven large villages in the southern part of Manipur were so severely affected that they were living on wild roots and soft leaves from the forest. We heard that the Christian villagers had made an agreement to have all things in common. Each day they shared whatever food was available. If they caught fish or crabs from the river, or killed a wild pig, fowl, rabbit, or even squirrels, they shared it with one another. If there was nothing but mushrooms, bamboo shoots, or wild roots, they shared that. "We are bound by a covenant to live together or to die together," the mission field superintendent reported.

Lord God, I prayed, *help me to help my people. Show me how I can raise money to buy rice for them during this emergency.* I wrote to twenty-five relief organizations asking for assistance for the seventy-five hundred Christian families who were facing the most severe famine. Before a response came we began hearing of deaths from starvation. Then a call came from Franklin Graham, head of the Samaritan's Purse organization.

"We have $15,000 for the project," he declared. Soon gifts came in from other Christian friends and we had enough for eight truckloads of rice.

My second son, John, and I flew to India to purchase the rice and oversee its distribution. When we finally reached Imphal, the largest city in Manipur, and the only one with an airport, we were greeted by my father and a whole busload of friends and relatives. They were all delighted to see John, for he had not visited the land of my birth for five years.

Our first order of business was to obtain permission from the chief minister to purchase rice from the government warehouse in Churachandpur.

"You are most certainly welcome to buy rice, *if* it is available," he told us. We drove the thirty-seven miles to Sielmat in three hours. This dirt road would be considered very rough by U.S. standards, but it is the best in the state.

The next morning I had a meeting with the field leaders of Partnership Mission Society, which operates eighty village schools for the mountain children, runs a small rural hospital and helps train national Christian leaders for the churches in the area. While I was tied up, I sent a friend to nearby Churachandpur to see if there was rice available at the government warehouse. All during the meeting I was trying hard to concentrate, but part of my mind was praying, *God, make the rice available. You've provided the money, but they can't eat money. Please, Lord, make it possible for us to find rice to purchase.*

When my friend returned I took one look at his smiling face and knew the report was favorable.

"The Deputy Commissioner said you are a very lucky man," he said with a smile. "If you had asked for rice yesterday, there would have been none. A good supply came in last evening. You may purchase as much as you can."

Everyone at the meeting was overjoyed at the news. Then the advice started: "It would be foolhardy for you to go to the interior hills;" "There are many landslides in the rainy season;" "You could be stranded for days;" "It is dangerous on those roads when they are muddy."

Sometimes I am not very good at taking advice. This was one of those times. John and I realized the roads would be treacherous, but we were determined to make the trip into the interior famine-stricken villages. We rented two trucks to haul rice and three jeeps to carry our team.

"Just think," I reminded my son, "when I was a small boy I traveled over these hills on foot. A trip that took me six days we now plan to drive in two days on the newly-constructed roads." Perhaps he had heard my stories too many times, because he decided to go in a different jeep with one of his Hmar cousins.

Wireless messages were sent to all the army camps throughout the hills so that, in case of emergency, they would assist us. Then we began our trip on the "jeepable" roads. "Jeepable" is a word my people have coined to describe the rough dirt roads that have been cut through the jungle. I found it quite appropriate.

We spent the next three days on the road, stopping at villages and distributing the rice among people who were pitifully appreciative. Many cried. Some had not eaten in days. It is the policy of the Partnership Mission Society to let the people work for their food, but the situation was so desperate that the rice was distributed in advance. We went from village to village unloading rice. When one truck became empty, we sent it back for more rice, then we would unload from the second truck until the first returned. This meant our crew was continually busy. We had less than five hours sleep each night. By the time we reached the end of the trail and had given out all the rice, we were exhausted.

The sky was heavily overcast as we prepared to make the return trip to Sielmat. Our drivers were concerned about the road, and with good reason. Just a few miles away a big landslide had almost eliminated the road. The border road crew had temporarily cleared it, but we navigated our jeeps over the piles of rocks and logs very gingerly.

We felt pressured to arrive at our destination before dark, because one of the jeeps had lost its headlights. To drive on the narrow, rut-filled roads along such deep crevices in the dark would be suicidal. We pushed on, in spite of the ceaseless rain.

At about four in the afternoon we were still sixty miles from Sielmat – three hour's journey. The first jeep rounded a curve and came to a sudden halt. A fresh landslide! The slide was still moving, and a creamy, liquid mud flowed onto the road from the pile of rocks and trees. With shovels and spades we dug our way out. The mud was still a foot deep on the road, but the first jeep made it through. John was in the second jeep, the one with no lights, and it followed close behind. As we attempted the crossing, the wet mud oozed into our jeep.

"Look at that thick, dark cloud coming our way," our driver worried out loud. "We must reach a safer place before that heavy rain reaches us." But there really was no safer place. We were moving at a snail's pace. Soon darkness fell, and we still had fifty miles to go.

We sandwiched the "blind" jeep and drove very slowly. I felt very uncomfortable about John being in the blind jeep, yet I dared not ask him to come with me. I didn't want to give the impression I thought John's life was more precious than the others'. We

125

began climbing a steep mountain that had many sharp curves; on the right were steep rocky gorges. The rain was pouring down so hard we could barely see the jeep in front of us. As we approached the most dangerous area where the gorges were the deepest and the road the most narrow, I held my breath. I could not hold out any longer and cried aloud, "Lord, do something! Bring back the lights on that jeep."

After another quarter of a mile or so, I told our driver to signal the blind jeep by flashing his lights on and off. Suddenly the lights of the blind jeep came on. We all honked our horns in praise to God. It was too wonderful for words!

It was nine-thirty when we pulled into our driveway in Sielmat. We found an anxious crowd waiting for us, including my aging parents. After a quick supper, the drivers were ready to return to their homes, but the blind jeep had again lost its lights.

"Leave it there for tonight and come with me," one of the other drivers suggested. "You can come back for it tomorrow."

Everyone left. The blind jeep stood there all alone in the darkness, an eloquent testimony of the fact that our God is a God of miracles. A God who is ever ready to help us. A God who can show us great and mighty things.